★

"Dayna really listened to the music. When we came to Houston, she came to the gigs. She did all the interviews. She was one of us. Dayna represents everything that is missing in the music industry today."

—**Earl Slick**, guitarist, David Bowie Band

★

"Having been in the music business for five decades, I can assure you the most interesting, volatile, productive, insane, and industry forming years were the late '70s through the '80s. There was no better or unique position to be in than AOR radio in those years, as you were able to interface with all the elements contributing to the madness that spawned the music industry as we know it. Dayna Steele, the face and voice of AOR radio in Houston, was part of it all. She knew the artists, their managers and agents, the promoters (a mad bunch in those days), and the record label personnel, all wanting a piece of the few precious hours Dayna was on the air. Therefore, she was involved in everything from artist development to artist disaster. I wish we still had the characters in the business like "those days," but sadly, "those days" are gone and but a memory set inside the brain of someone like Dayna. Not many of those stories have seen the light of day but when they do . . . wow!"

—**Troy Blakely**, APA Talent and Literary Agency

★

"Dayna has an uncanny ability to turn an uncommon concept into a productive operation into a viable corporation—and create something of value—in any field she chooses. From her early rock-star days of fame in Houston as the voice of the Steeleworkers, Dayna knows what people want and how to bring it to them. I was a loyal Steeleworker, listening to Dayna while training for missions in space. Dayna will always be out-of-this-world!"

—**Jim Wetherbee**, NASA Space Shuttle Commander

★

"Nobody markets themselves or their businesses quite like the top rock-and-roll bands. Dayna has taken those techniques and recorded them in an entertaining and informative book. *Rock to the Top* is Guerilla Marketing to the tune of rock and roll!"

—**Jay Conrad Levinson**, author of the *Guerrilla Marketing* series of books

★

"This book rocks. Dayna definitely paid attention during all those record company dinners in her radio days. I guarantee she will never eat alone!"

—**Keith Ferrazzi**, author of *Never Eat Alone*

★

"In this wonderfully entertaining book, Dayna Steele proves that you can find great business lessons almost anywhere—provided you know what to look for. *Rock to the Top* is a rockin' good way to hone your entrepreneurial skills."

—**Bo Burlingham**, *Inc.* magazine editor-at-large and author of *Small Giants: Companies That Choose to Be Great Instead of Big*

★

"Dayna Steele is a friend to many in the rock star category because she always paid attention to the important stuff with artists. More than just a radio personality or executive, Dayna is a human being with a sensitivity to others that transcends the mundane and reaches to improve the quality of life for others."

—**Bill Siddons**, manager for The Doors, Crosby Stills & Nash, and Alice in Chains

★

"At the beginning of my acting career, I cleaned pools in Houston to pay the bills. Listening to Dayna on my Walkman, tuned to KLOL, was the only thing that got me through those days. I listened to her every day! It was cool when I had the chance to meet her years later during a broadcast in New York City."

—**Frank Dicopoulos**, 'Frank Cooper' on CBS's *Guiding Light*

★

"Dayna was hands-down one of the most influential rock programmers of the late '80s."

—**Bill Leopold**, WFL Management, Melissa Etheridge

★

"Dayna was the musical brains behind one of the top-three most influential rock stations in the '80s. She broke rock bands!!!!!! I wish I had a hundred dollars for every time, as a promotion man, I said, 'Dayna Steele added it at KLOL' . . . and another hundred for each add I got behind her action. Dayna was a leader."

—**Bill McGathy**, In De Goot Entertainment: Sinedown, Chevelle, Puddle of Mudd, Saliva, Black Stone Cherry

★

"Dayna taught me a lot about etiquette. She was always very appreciative of everything and anything someone else might do on her behalf. She was very quick with a handwritten thank-you card—a rarity in a business where much is expected and little acknowledged. To this day, I now follow the same good manners."

—**Ronnie Raphael**, SWAN Marketing and Management

ROCK
TO THE TOP

**WHAT I
LEARNED ABOUT
SUCCESS
FROM THE
WORLD'S GREATEST
ROCK STARS**

Classic business advice to the tune of rock and roll!

DAYNA STEELE

**Award Winning Rock Radio Personality
and Successful Entrepreneur**

BROWN BOOKS   DALLAS, TEXAS

ROCK TO THE TOP

WHAT I LEARNED ABOUT SUCCESS FROM THE WORLD'S GREATEST ROCK STARS

© 2008 Steele Media Services
Cover photos by Evin Thayer and www.rockhardcases.com
Other photos courtesy of Gary Bankhead, Theresa DiMenno, Phyllis Hand,
Bruce Kessler, and www.healthandfitnessmag.com
About the author photo by Russ Fortson

LYRIC CREDITS

Sammy Hagar: *There's Only One Way To Rock*—Special thanks to Sammy Hagar

The Kinks: *Celluloid Heroes*—Sony/ATV Music Publishing, LLC

Rush: *Roll the Bones*—SRO Management/Anthem Entertainment

Scorpions: *No Pain No Gain*—Universal Music Publishing Group

Bon Jovi: *Fear*— Universal Music Publishing Group

Lynyrd Skynyrd: *What's Your Name*—Universal Music Publishing Group

Joan Jett: *Desire*—Special thanks to Joan Jett and Kenny Laguna

Heart: *Anything Is Possible*—Dalbello Toonz & Universal Music Group

The Who: *My Generation*—The Richmond Organization

ZZ Top: *I Thank You*—Rondor Music International/Universal Music Publishing Group/Alfred Music o/b/o Warner/Chappell Music, Inc.

Bachman-Turner Overdrive: *You Ain't Seen Nothin' Yet*—Sony/ATV Music Publishing, LLC

Manufactured in the United States of America

For information, please contact:

Brown Books Publishing Group
16200 North Dallas Parkway, Suite 170
Dallas, Texas 75248
www.brownbooks.com
972-381-0009

A New Era in Publishing™

ISBN-13: 978-1-934812-06-8
ISBN-10: 1-934812-06-4
LCCN: 2007942356

1 2 3 4 5 6 7 8 9 10

This book is dedicated to

Alison "The Nightbird" Steele

Molly Smyth

Ed Leffler

There would have been no stories without them.

And to

Cathy Forsythe

I'm positive she already has
an intern for me in heaven.

Itinerary:

Table of Contents

★

Gene Simmons:

Foreword

★

Rock and roll is great. The fringe benefits are great. The money is great. But rock and roll is hard work, and to be successful you have to treat it like a business.

It's not enough to be lucky—you have to make your own luck. There are so many crucial things that go into being successful in business. I know exactly what I've had to do to go this far. I work hard and long. I'm on time. I look for opportunities. I return calls. I keep notes. I'm organized.

Dayna has spent years learning and developing profitable business practices that she's just giving away in this book. I'll tell you that whatever you are doing, time is what you've got to work with. Effort is also a huge contributing factor to success, but the most important thing you need to put in is time. The more time you invest into something, the more successful you will be. So, what I do is, I work seven days a week. I don't take vacations. I work weekends, days, and nights—all so I can put in more time. I'm sober. And I don't sleep all that much, but when I do, I sleep sound.

Rock stars may know how to live it up, but to get to

the level where KISS is, requires sacrifices and business savvy. It's the hours and hours of work offstage that make a show great. It requires planning and precision. This book offers an enormous inside look into what makes or breaks a band and has translated that into universal principles for success in any business.

Rock bands, by and large, don't do licensing and merchandising well or work hard for that matter. KISS was never one of those bands. Because of our tireless efforts, KISS did, does, and always will achieve more than any other band out there. The proof is the fans. We give them what they want. And commercialism is good because it means somebody wants to buy your stuff. If you're lucky, you're not just a band, you're a brand.

Rock to the Top shows how far confidence, passion, quality, market awareness, and appropriate use of pyrotechnics can take anyone. These are all things I have continually invested in KISS and in all of my other areas of business. I didn't start out at the top, but I did put myself there. And anyone can do the same.

Dayna may be willing to divulge all her secrets, but this is the only free thing I'll give you, and I'm only going to say it one more time. Work hard. That's it. You can read *Rock to the Top* and figure out the rest of it. Or hire me to do it for you. I'm expensive but worth it.

—Gene Simmons

Gene Simmons co-founded KISS with Paul Stanley thirty-four years ago. KISS has since been the #1 gold-record, award-winning group in America (RIAA) and has broken box office records around the world, set by Elvis and The Beatles. For three decades they have continued to be the juggernaut of licensing and merchandising.

Outside of KISS, Simmons discovered Van Halen, managed Liza Minnelli's recording career, and created, produced, co-hosted, and co-starred in multiple film and television productions, including A&E's *Gene Simmons' Family Jewels* and a dozen other TV projects, such as *Trophy Wife*, to air soon.

Simmons is the author of two *New York Times* best-sellers: *KISS and Make-up* (Crown Books) and *Sex Money KISS* (Simmons/ Phoenix Books) and has established his own publishing imprints— Simmons Books, Simmons Audio Visual, and Simmons Records.

Road Crew:

Acknowledgments

★

Ladies and gentlemen,
would you please welcome . . . .

A successful band can't do a show without a superb road crew, and I could not have put this book and this life together without my own great crew. If I have forgotten a name, please forgive me. It was the '80s and it was a wild time.

To my Steeleworkers: the fans who listened, cheered, made this all possible, and kept asking for the stories to be told again and again.

To the DJs, program directors, music directors, general managers, sales staff, interns, concert promoters, and other personnel along the way, including Jeff Lowe, Doc Morgan, Michael Jones, Bill Todd, Blake Lawrence, Jackie McCauley, Charlie Weiss, Jay Isbell, Rick Lambert, Roger W. Garrett, Michelle Sayre, Jay Jones, Ken Anthony, Brian Shannon, Miss Lilly Bunyard, Charlie Peña, Ed Levine, Brian the Butler, George and Sylvia Flavin, Garth

"Hemp" Kemp, Pat Fant, Mark Masters, Bart Taylor, Hannah Storm, Moby, John Alan, Bill Cordell, Sig Izbrand, John Allen, Denton Marr, Kaz, Ted Edwards, Bill Moffett, the Colonel, Cindy Bennett Smith, Trish Clement, Donna McKenzie, Cindy Spicer, the interns who got lunch, Lanny and Debbie Griffith, Harvey Kojan, Martha Martinez, Grego, Linda Silk, Crash, Nick Van Cleve, Jeff Jensen, Jim Pruett, Mark Stevens, Dave Andrews, Frank the Guard, Tena Clark, Kevin Dorsey, Kit Wall, Karl Van Kyle, Ed Beauchamp, Cathy Pletcher-Baker-Boyd-Harrison-Clapton-Candlestickmaker, Muriel Funches, Louie Messina, all the Beckers, Viva Harris, Greg Dodson, Jean and Robert Martinez, Jeannie McKinney, Mark Moss, and Chris Miller. And to Andy Beaubien who kicked me out of the nest. I taught myself to fly.

To the brilliant Doug Harris who could give P.T. Barnum a run for his money.

To John Michael Provenzano, Marko Babineau, Bubba Wayne, Rhonda Rose, Al Matthias, Bill McGathy, Michael Stevens, Ronnie Raphael, Sammy Alfano, Rod Tanner, Charlie Minor, Skip Bishop, Tommy Chaltas, Johnny Hughes, Grant Guthrie, Norman Hurt, Texas Tapes & Records, Mark Niederhauser, Meredyth Hayes, Sharon Lepere, Lisa Giles, Colleen MacDonald Taylor, Rhonda Beasley, Jon Matthews, Anne Marie Foley, Phil Poulos, Fred Meyers, June Colbert, George Weinberg, Brad Hunt, Barney Kilpatrick, Tom Murphy, Drew Murray, Heavy Lenny, Rob Sides, Doug Mattice, Murray Nagle, Hershell Orr, Paul Pieretti, Todd Galli, and all the other record reps for all the shows, meals, interviews, records-then-CDs, tickets, trips, and backstage passes. They were always appreciated.

To the photographers who were there to document it: Gary Bankhead, Bruce Kessler, Phyllis Hand, and Teresa Dimenno.

To dear friends who stepped forward to help me with facts, advice, and more on several occasions: Doc McGhee, Bill Siddons, Bill Leopold, Tom Consolo, Patti Martin and Patty Martin, Tommy Nast, Joe Cerisano, Julie Rader, and Earl Slick—all gems who actually returned phone calls.

To Jeanie and Ayn for a great place to live.

To agent extraordinaire Troy Blakely. Damn, that was a lot of money for playing records.

To the amazing Susan McCoy Neuhalfen for her tireless efforts at editing my stories.

To Gwen Griffin who gave me the confidence to move forward.

To everyone at Brown Books for such amazing support.

To my "in-laws"—Cody, Alan, and Brenda—who said, "you should write a book."

To the wonderful Justiz clan—who love me despite the fact that I make it rain in Miami.

To my Nicholson family—Mom, Dad, Scooter, Kathy, Lorelle, and Madison.

To the loves of my life—Cris, Dack, and Nick. They are better than any backstage pass or front row ticket.

And to my best friend—Charlie the Wonder Husband. Enough said.

The Opening Act:

Prologue

★

"Did you used to be somebody?"

Dack Justiz

For almost two decades, I ruled the radio airwaves in Houston, Texas, as the city's anointed "First Lady of Radio." Ratings shares were at astronomical highs, concert tickets were free, and I was eventually making well into six figures to play some of the greatest rock music ever released. I hung out with rock stars and celebrities. I was quoted in newspapers and industry magazines across the globe, and I was often featured on television. The radio microphone opened doors all over the world for anything I wanted or needed.

Limos and private jets became a part of my life. Super bands were flying me across the country for national album releases. There were live broadcasts from places like New York, Los Angeles, and Las Vegas. Tens of thousands of fans, who referred to themselves as *Steeleworkers*, cheered as

I emceed major rock events year after year. The credentials read "VIP" wherever I went, whether it was the original Live Aid concert in Philadelphia or the opening of The Hard Rock Hotel in Vegas. In 1996, *Billboard Magazine* nominated me as one of five "Local Radio Personalities of the Year" across the country. I was the only woman in the category. I was at the top.

Yet many were surprised when I moved on and successfully transitioned from that world to the world of business. I created and sold a profitable e-commerce venture; started a marketing and public relations firm; and most recently, founded *Smart Girls Rock*, an online community for girls who will be the next leaders, scientists, mathematicians, and engineers. Through it all, I've always gone back to the great lessons I learned from my amazing, and sometimes outrageous, experiences with the world's greatest rock bands.

A few days after my seventeenth birthday, I left for college with a car, an apartment lease, a college ID, and not a clue what I wanted to be when I grew up. All I knew was that I wanted to be a "star" at something, and I was determined to be on my way.

With initial classes aimed towards pre-med, I became a student at Texas A&M University. Now, keep in mind I can't stand the sight of blood and have never been a fan of science, but it seemed like a lofty goal and sounded fairly impressive as well to my parents and anyone else who cared to ask.

Within weeks it was obvious that medicine, and perhaps college, was not my passion. As I walked through the
student center during another uneventful day in my early
college career, I came upon the university theater group.
The Aggie Players were pitching anyone who looked their
way, signing up students for everything from auditions to
stage building.

I had spent my three years in high school with Dis-
tributive Education (a business group that allowed me to
get a real job and leave school after lunch each day) and
the rest of my time with the theater group (they were fun
and looked cool and smoked cigarettes in the school parking lot without getting caught). I was never an actress,
but I ran the lights for each production, gaining a love of
backstage and everything that went on there. The Aggie
Players hooked another one that day.

Signing up as a lighting technician, I spent most evenings trying to look cool and smoking cigarettes where no
one cared. It was becoming fairly clear, probably by my
grades, that I wasn't exactly destined to be a doctor. Then
during one of those productive evenings of "hanging out,"
a friend of a friend who happened to be a local disc jockey,
and thus a *huge* star in College Station, Texas, mentioned
that he had heard that the university was starting a student
radio station and was looking for disc jockeys to train. A
dare was thrown out: who was brave enough to audition?

I was bored, trying to find reasons not to go to class,
and hoping the disc jockey who had thrown down the dare

would ask me out, so I took the challenge and the next morning went in search of whoever was in charge. As I was the only female student who had inquired and eagerly agreed to take the worst shifts available, I was hired on the spot. No pay, no college credit, horrible hours, but a chance to say, "Why yes, I am on the radio." Looking back, I'm not sure if that initial dare was actually meant for me, the group, or someone else all together. Nonetheless, the disc jockey didn't ask me out, but his dare changed my life.

From the moment I put on the headphones, I knew I was home. I knew what it meant to have a passion for something. Along the way, I filed records, swept floors, and hung out trying to get noticed by management. I did weekend shifts, overnight shifts, morning and after-noon drives, and midday shifts. From overnights, playing records in a closet, to center stage, as one of the highest rated (and highest paid) female rock and roll disc jockeys in the country, I watched the most successful people I was exposed to on a daily basis—the rock stars, the huge bands, and their management personnel—and tried to figure out how they had made it to the top. That was where I wanted to be.

As my career evolved over the years from rock and roll air personality to a successful entrepreneur, I could always trace it all back to the basics I learned from the world's greatest rock stars: from the importance of confidence and quality to knowledge and branding. They not only made great music, they also made great sense.

I Love Rock and Roll:

Passion

★

"There's only one way to rock."

Sammy Hagar

There are a lot of recordings that never receive airplay and concert tickets that remain unsold, but despite that, bands keep recording and keep touring. It's what they love and can't stop doing. They have a passion for the music.

Passion. You can't buy it, borrow it, steal it, or fake it. Passion is found within. You won't learn how to have passion from this book. You either have a passion for something or you don't. And, if you don't, you need to stop what you are doing, take stock of your life, and figure out what it is you really want to do, what really makes you happy. You may not be able to do it now, but you can take the steps and knowledge gained from this book to work towards the goal of a home-based business, life as a ski instructor, being the world's greatest stockbroker, or whatever it is you want to do.

The fact that you bought this book means you have a passion for something. Maybe it's being successful in business or maybe you love rock and roll. Either way, it is a good start. And isn't passion how great relationships start anyway? What do you really want to do? Can you possibly imagine doing anything else and being happy? Will you enjoy the moment when people ask what you do and you have the chance to tell them?

Passion is satisfaction with a job well done, knowing that it is your hard work and creativity that brings a product or service to fruition. You just have to realize that there won't always be passion on a daily basis, and there will be repetition of tedious tasks. Just ask any band who has had to play the same songs, night after night, for just enough money to pay the crew and buy dinner. Again, you have to love what you do.

When I left rock radio, Bill Moffett, voiceover artist and production guru, gave me a framed copy of the single for Led Zeppelin's "Stairway to Heaven" with a quote from my last day on the air, "I'll never have to play Stairway to Heaven again." Obviously, it is a brilliant piece of music that still stands the test of time today. I was just happy to never play it ever again in my entire life. I must have played that song one hundred thousand times in my career. The funny thing is that when my firstborn came into the world, I didn't know any nursery rhymes. I hadn't exactly been steeped in that music genre the last fifteen years. When he

*would get fussy, the only thing I could think of to sing when
I leaned over the crib was, yeah you guessed it, ". . . and
she's buuuu-yyyyy-iinnngggg the stairway to heaven."*

Still can't find your passion or define it? You'll know
it when it happens, just like the first time I put on those
headphones. Jazz musician Diana Krall has a great TV ad
where she is talking about hearing a piece of music for
the first time. She was so moved by that piece of music
that, for her, playing the piano was the only way she could
express her emotions. Look at her face. *That* is passion. Or
phenomenal acting.

★ We Are the Champions

Tennis legend Billie Jean King once said at a speech
I emceed that "everyone desires to be a champion but
very few have the desire to do the work it takes to be a
champion." Passion gives you energy. Passion makes you
work hard and give it your all. You have to love what you
do so that you jump out of bed each day and look forward
to the day and what it may bring. And you have to be
willing to work hard for what it is you want. If you love
what you do, hard work shouldn't be a problem. You'll
put in the effort to succeed and enjoy the journey no
matter how steep the hill.

*My first gig at a major market radio station was
weekends, fill-ins, and overnight–whatever was needed–at*

KRLY-FM, known as "Y94", in Houston, Texas. The sta-
tion was a hip, cool, album-oriented rock station (AOR),
and was full of good-looking, hip, and cocky male DJs. I
attempted to assume their swagger and smart-ass attitude
almost immediately. Fortunately, that lasted all of a week
or so when the hippest and coolest of them all, Doc Mor-
gan, took me to the side and said, "Hey kid, it may look
like we are having fun, and we are, but we have all worked
our butts off to get where we are, and it will be no different
for you." He eloquently went on to add, "Quit f******
off, and remember that ultimately this is a business, and
if you want to make it in this business, you will treat it as
one and earn everything you get."

I took that advice to heart and started the hard work.
I filed records day and night until I never wanted to see
another record album again. I took every shift offered
without complaint. And I was at the station for hours on
end just in case something needed to be done. I think they
finally gave me a full-time shift just so they could get me
out of the halls and trap me in that little studio, where I
was out of the way, for hours at a time.

★ The Fever

When you have passion for a business or a project, it
can be very contagious to those around you if you let that
passion show. And those are the people you want. Your
co-workers and/or employees should be exposed to that

passion each and every day. Let them know your vision and your goals for the business. In addition, you must allow them to be a part of that passion, make their own suggestions, and occasionally implement their new ideas. When others catch on to your passion, when they feel they are part of something, they in turn will work hard on what you are creating. It becomes a group effort or a group passion. On that same note, if you are stingy and keep it all to yourself, refusing to use their ideas and help, it will work against you and your passion. I'd rather have one person working *with* me than have three working *for* me. It makes all the difference in the world.

Tonya Middleton, General Manager of my out-of-this-world e-commerce effort called the Space Store, was just as passionate about our business as I was, as the owner. In fact, I think there were times she took it all more personally than I did. She said, "Dayna trusted me to do what was right even when she was not there. With that trust, came my love for the job and why I ran the store like it was mine. That trust also made me believe in myself. And, I wanted to see the store grow and succeed because I knew that with Dayna we could have a great business." When I sold the company to Spacehab Inc., a NASA contractor, Tonya and I continued to work just as hard and be just as proud because it was a success story we both had created.

In 1985, KLOL began conducting Rock and Roll Auctions. The first two were held in a record store in a local mall. After those successes, the auctions moved to a popular nightclub, then to the parking lot of the Hard Rock Café. Outgrowing this rock venue sent us to The Summit, one of the largest arenas in Houston. Going from raising just over one thousand dollars to raising well over one hundred thousand dollars, when the last auction was held, the KLOL auction became famous. That fame included not only the quality of items and rock stars involved but also the passion it evoked from those participating. Salaried employees put in countless unpaid hours, and normally jaded rock stars worked their butts off trying to out-do each other, not only as auctioneers but also as donators of the highest priced rock memorabilia. It was the passion all of us had for the auction that made it such a success, and we spread that passion to others.

★ Don't Let the Sun Go Down on Me

Passion is powerful. It is powerful enough to overcome obstacles and powerful enough to create a few. Although I never had more than a passing introduction to Rick Allen, drummer for rock superstars Def Leppard, I always found him to be an inspiration for what passion can do. Here is a band member, a drummer no less, who lost one arm in a horrible car accident in late 1984. It could have, and should have, meant the end of his career and possibly the band's demise. Instead, he made some changes to the drum set, added some custom innovations, and taught himself to play with the one arm he had left. He has released six albums since with Def Leppard and played to rave reviews.

Whether you are finding a way to keep the band going with a one-armed drummer or finding a way to pull more customers out of a hat, passion will keep you going and keep you coming up with new ideas and innovations. However, passion is powerful enough to pull you over to the dark side of drugs, alcohol, and embezzlement as seen in a few band members and Enron executives. Fortunately, passion can pull you back to the right side as well.

One of those early rock and roll auctions we held in a local record store gave me my first opportunity to work with Steven Tyler of Aerosmith. The band had just successfully come out of rehab and was trying to get out and get established as a top rock and roll band once again. Charlie Weiss, KLOL newsman, and I decided to stand on the counter with Steven, Joan Jett, and a host of others at the auction to raise money for charity. Aerosmith hadn't been out of rehab long, and this was one of the first appearances band members were making in their new sober life with a new album under their belts. Steven came by the celebration party later that evening at my apartment and talked about how great it was to be back out with the fans. He commented to me that getting straight was the only choice he had to keep what he really loved: Aerosmith. These days, some regard Aerosmith as the greatest American rock and roll band of all time. It simply took a passion for the job.

★ Girls, Girls, Girls

Passion helps you to ignore the word, "no."

This particular advice is for women, but the men are welcome to stick around as well. We've come a long way, baby, but we still have a ways to go. You will have to work harder to get to the top, and you might not always make as much as a man in the same position. Stop complaining. Get over it. If you really have a passion for what you are doing, identify the problem and find or create a solution. And do your job better than anyone else, male or female. Joan Jett never stopped trying to be a rock star, despite numerous rejections, and she is still a rock star to this day. Although it was said time and time again, Heart's Ann and Nancy Wilson never would listen to anyone say two chicks couldn't have one of the greatest rock bands of all time. Complaints will never break the glass ceiling, but passion will. You simply use your passion and work through the problem or glass ceiling.

Radio is not much different today than it was in the late 1980s. Most stations had one woman on the air, usually doing a midday or evening shift. Rarely did you hear a woman in prime drive times in the morning and afternoon. When KLOL was riding particularly high one rating season, I was the token woman doing middays, with a lesser-rated male disc jockey doing afternoons and getting all the glory, not to mention the better paid personal appearances.

Instead of moping around and complaining, I put together the facts and figures and then made an appointment with the General Manager. In a calm and professional manner, I presented this information to him. I asked, "Why is he doing afternoons and I am doing middays, when I have higher ratings and better recognition among our listeners?" The GM had never even considered moving me, a woman, to afternoon drive. Once he was presented with the fact that my higher ratings translated into higher ad revenue, he took action. I grabbed the reins of afternoon drive the following Monday. Instead of feeling sorry for myself and complaining that my glass ceiling was caused by the fact that I was a woman, I took my passion and found a solution to the problem.

★ Changes

There will be days you don't love what you do. That is normal. But when those days turn into weeks which then into months, it's time to take a long, hard look at what is going on in your life and with your passion.

Passion can change. There are signs inward and outward, from your brain, your body, your network, and your co-workers. This is where you need to pay attention and know when it is time to make those changes. A couple of years ago, I created and hosted *The Art of Doing Business* on the BizRadio Network. Here is a list I put together: The Top Ten Signs It's Time to Look for Another Job.

1. Your last bonus was smaller than everyone else's bonus.

2. Others are being promoted over you.

3. You know what really makes you happy and this is not it.

4. You are only doing enough to get by.

5. You are not excited about what the day ahead may hold for you.

6. Your job or business is making you sick from the stress, or there is a pit in your stomach at just the thought of going to work.

7. The day crawls by and you're bored to death.

8. You are not included in important meetings.

9. Your boss is avoiding you.

10. When people ask what you do, you aren't really excited to tell them.

This list applies to passion. Did any of it make you think or hesitate? Did I hit a nerve? Be honest and truthful with yourself. Are you doing or getting ready to do what you really want to do? If the answer is no, then put the book down and go off somewhere and think. Where and when are you the happiest on any given day? Not giddy-happy but contented-happy. Ultimately, only you can come up with an answer to that question.

If you resoundingly say, "yes," without hesitation to what it is you are doing, then you have the passion, and you are well on your way to a successful business and life.

Passion

★ Plus hard work equals success

★ Is contagious to others

★ Overcomes barriers and obstacles

★ Gives you the energy to keep going

★ Blocks out the words "no" and "you can't"

★ Leads you down the right path

Why Yes, I Am a Rock Star:

Confidence

★

"Everybody's a star."

The Kinks

R arely does a rock star walk into a room and modestly say, "I am *just* a rock star." No, they swagger and command your attention because they are *stars*, seemingly larger-than-life. Now, I'll let you in on a little secret I learned from watching many rock stars backstage: they put their spandex pants on one leg at a time, and some of them are really some of the most insecure people I have ever met.

However, they have learned how to overcome their fears, or at least to appear confident when it counts. Right before they walk onstage, their shoulders go back, they get a determined look in their eyes, and then they make their grand entrance into the glittering floodlights as if the stage was built solely for them and no one else.

No matter what your calling, you can adopt that same level of confidence in business or in life. You can learn to visualize yourself as a rock star, as that successful person taking command of the stage in your life.

You have a passion for whatever it is you want to do. Now all we need to do is build up your confidence and turn you into that rock star. Confidence will be a big part of your success, and it is important that you make the audience believe in you. If you believe in yourself, others will believe in you as well. And like passion, confidence is contagious.

★ Don't Fear the Reaper

Bands will have unflattering reviews and there will be days the critics can be brutal. There were times the Houston press loved me and there were the other times where they could write something so biting it hurt. I was, and still am, a huge fan of columnist Ken Hoffman, first with the Houston Post (may it rest in peace) and now with the Houston Chronicle. But he could be catty when he wanted to make a point. He once wrote, when I left 97 Talk in Houston, "This is the third time she's quit radio, tying her with the Judds, the Who, and Frank Sinatra for most show business retirements without actually leaving." At least I was mentioned in good company.

You can't worry about what people think, and you can't be shy about what it is you do or the product you offer. If it is what you want to do, you can't stop thinking about it and you just know it would work, then you have to at least try it.

I can't tell you how many people expected me to fail miserably at talk radio, but within a year I had been named to the 1998 *Talkers Magazine's* 100 Most Important Radio Talk Show Hosts. When I left radio altogether to start the Space Store, the consensus again was that I had lost my mind. The Space Store became the largest e-commerce venture of its type, and I sold it to a NASA aerospace contractor for a nice profit several years after I started it. Crazy, but it worked.

The audience can't hear you if you don't sing. Shout it out to the world. Make sure everyone knows about you and your product or service, whether they are the neighbor, family, mail carrier, or dry cleaner. We'll talk about that more with networking, but make sure you always have a business card. When someone asks what you do, proudly and confidently tell them. The more you promote you and your product or service, the more everyone begins to think you are on to something. And everybody likes to jump on board with a winner.

I knew if I was going to make a name for myself, I was going to have to command attention when I went to appearances, from car lots to amusement parks. I came up with an outrageous outfit that consisted of a long sleeved black leotard, fishnet stockings, black heels, and a tuxedo jacket with the bow tie to match. It seems embarrassing now, but it was attention getting then. I was confident that it was cool and sexy. I was also confident that if I could get their attention, they would listen to me on the radio. I knew I could win over the audience there.

★ Physical Graffiti

Swagger, strut, hold your shoulders back, look people in the eye, and give a firm handshake. Energy gives off an aura of confidence. No matter how nervous or unsettled you are prior to an important meeting, speech, or presentation, energy can make up for a lot until you find your footing. Take a big breath, walk into the meeting or out on the stage, look at your audience, greet them in a strong, sure voice, and take command of that particular stage. You'll gain confidence with each and every minute.

The Rolling Stones' Mick Jagger probably does it better than anyone. He knows he is a rock star, but he didn't start out as a rock star. I'd like to imagine that, in the beginning, he kept waiting for someone to walk up to him and say, "Hey, you're not a rock star. You're just a short, geeky guy from the London School of Economics." Yes, the Rolling Stones backed it all up with great music, but let's face it, to this day you can't take your eyes off Mick.

Mick Jagger was doing a rare telephone interview to promote a solo project. I had planned, prepared, and looked forward to this interview for several weeks. Mick called a little early and, since I couldn't put him on the air immediately, I had to put him on hold. When I did pick up the phone, I was laughing and said, "last week I hung up on Robert Plant and this week I put Mick Jagger on hold." With somewhat of a smile in his voice, Jagger said, "Well, you wouldn't have been puttin' me on hold for very long on that thing." There were two very confident people on the phone that day. By the way, legend has is that Mick was actually asked to leave the London School of Economics in his first year after riding a motorcycle through the library. That is something you do when you are definitely confident that there is another career on the horizon.

As simple as it sounds, the way you physically hold yourself will make a difference in what people think of you and your service or product. All is judged by that first impression. Standing up straight with your shoulders back and looking people in the eye isn't all that difficult to do. You simply remember to do it every time until it becomes a habit. To this day, I occasionally have someone ask, "are you somebody?" It's not because I have an entourage, or drive an expensive car, or even wear expensive clothes. It's all in the way I carry myself. I've done it for years and it is habit now.

★ Lucky Man

Musicians send demo after demo to record companies, only to be shot down most of the time. Linkin Park, a current record-charting rock band, was told their music would never work. It just wouldn't sell. Led Zeppelin was told their music was so bad that it would go over like a lead zeppelin.

Even with all the confidence in the world, you may

have to apply persistence to the equation as well. I applied several times for positions at KLOL-FM in Houston, being turned away as too young and/or too inexperienced each time. Except the *last* time. I was finally in the right place at the right time, and there was an opening for a deejay on the late night shift. I found a home for fourteen years.

In the mid-1980s, Silver Condor, though not exactly a household name in the world of rock music, enjoyed a brief stint in the limelight. They traveled across the country, performing, doing interviews, and all those things rock stars do. Lead singer Joe Cerisano, who started in the business at fourteen, told me about how many times he sent in tapes and tried to jumpstart his rock career. "You get to the point where you go down the road so far that you can't turn back. It's farther back than it is to go forward, and all the while, you're getting better at what you do. I had rejection slips from Columbia Records nine years before I signed my deal with them. I saved them to remind me if I ever needed to be reminded," Joe said. "Call it blind faith or naiveté. I'm not sure what it is, but if you go for it, you never have to wonder what might have been because you tried. The amount of success is all relative to what success means to you."

Joe never stopped trying. As defeated as he could feel sometimes in a tough business, he always threw those shoulders back and walked into the next record company to try again. And believe me, Joe's stuff was good (and *still is). So good, in fact, that after Silver Condor, Joe was offered the job as lead singer of Black Sabbath, one of the top rock bands in the world. And you know what? Joe had the confidence to know it wasn't what he wanted to do, and said, "Thank you, but no thank you." Some people may have thought that meant he failed, but Joe just took it all as a learning experience and moved on from there. He went on to become a very successful jingle writer and singer. Perhaps you have heard one of his "hits" for the U.S. Army. "Be All That You Can Be." That's confidence.*

Confidence can be the ability to recognize the right path for you even if it doesn't appear to be the most obvious route to quick success. Confidence can also be the instinct to sense opportunity that isn't apparent to others.

A long-time record rep in Houston, Patti Martin, once said, "Dayna, no matter how many things you try, and no matter how many times you fall on your face, you are amazing. None of it fazes you. You just keep trying."

Patti also once gave me *There Must Be a Pony*, a book which I cherish because it truly sums up my philosophy. I'll give you the short version, which is somewhat like the glass half full, half empty analogy, only better. In this story, there are two brothers who come upon a barn filled to the rafters with horse manure. One brother says, "There's nothing but poo in there," and he leaves. The other brother sees an opportunity and says, "But, there must be a pony!"

To this day, in anything I take on, I am confident that there is a pony. I'm just going to have to work to get to it and dig through a lot of poo.

★ We Gotta Get Out of This Place

Sometimes a song, no matter how hard you work on it, just isn't going to be a hit. It's just not. No matter what. But, it is only considered a failure if you learn absolutely nothing from the experience.

> In 1990, I announced I was leaving radio to move to Los Angeles and try my hand at acting, something I had always fantasized about doing. I basically spent ten months living on credit cards and auditioning for a living, which is not very lucrative. There are those around me who to this day still refer to it as the time I failed in Los Angeles. However, I have never looked at it as failing because I learned so much. I learned not to live on credit cards ever again. I learned I can try anything and survive. I learned that Los Angeles is not all happy, shiny, famous people. And I learned I can't act my way out of a box.

Confidence will give you the courage to try new things and some just flat-out won't work. I never became an actress and had a short-lived television career. Even the first few months of talk radio were awful. But I kept turning on that mic and trying. You can't let failure take away your confidence. Fight it and learn from it. The more you try new things, the more you'll learn, the more experience you'll gain, and the more contacts you'll make. And that leads to great confidence.

★ While My Guitar Gently Weeps

Develop a thick skin, but don't run over people. It's okay to say, "Hey, look at me and my accomplishments." You're going to have to do that when people ask what you do and when you talk to the press, but don't start believing your own press. Be confident and pleasant to be around, not confident and overbearing. I know, since I attempted that move a few times and fell flat on my face as well as burning a few bridges along the way. A little appreciation (more on that in another chapter) and humble pie go a long way.

The Ovation Guitar Company was kind enough to offer me a beautiful Ovation 6-string acoustic guitar to keep around in case someone ever wanted to play live on the air (I guess we were the predecessor to MTV Unplugged; we just didn't know it at the time). Anyway, I can't play a note to save my life on the thing, but it looked good next to my desk, and I was (and still am) quite proud of it. It is a beautiful instrument. Since I had so many musicians and performers in and out of my office and the studio in those days, I thought it would make a great collectible if I had the artists sign it as they dropped by, especially those who played it. It was a brilliant idea except I didn't keep a list of who signed it, and I still can't decipher most of the signatures to this day.

I do remember one signature, and I still sneer at it every time I walk by the guitar in our living room. Steve Miller, the original space cowboy, was just a little too confident and cocky when asked to sign the guitar. He grabbed the guitar, yanked the pen out of my hand, ignored my plea to keep it small so many others could sign, and took up a good portion of the bottom right side of my prized piece of memorabilia. I have yet to forgive him. And you know what? From that point on, when faced with two songs to play on the radio and time to play only one, a Steve Miller song always got put back in the queue.

★ Who Are You?

Remember, if you believe you are a rock star, the audience will believe you are a rock star. Sometimes, most of the time, confidence is just acting confident. The actual confidence will follow later.

To this day, when I walk on a stage in front of an audience, I am Dayna Steele, sure of myself with a commanding voice. Inside, I am Dayna Nicholson, the geeky and gawky girl from Dulles High School, waiting for someone to call me out. I still shake prior to and after an appearance, speech, or emcee event. Somewhere in the middle, Dayna Steele takes over and I just let her go. From early on, I believed in Dayna Steele and soon others did as well.

Thomas Edison once said, "If we did all the things we're capable of doing, we would literally astonish ourselves." If you back up that newfound confidence with the other steps in this book, you'll have a firm foundation for whatever you decide to take on. You really can do anything you set your mind to.

Confidence

★ Don't worry what other people think

★ Look and act confident, the actual confidence
will follow

★ Never give up, keep trying

★ Failure is not the end of something,
merely a lesson

★ Confidence does not equal rudeness

★ You believe and your audience will believe

Make It a Multi-Platinum Seller:
Quality

★

"Good work is the key to good fortune."
Rush

A band can spend days, weeks, even months or years in the studio perfecting their next recording into a quality product to be recorded onto a CD and then ultimately, downloaded into your iPod. It takes a lot of people working together, doing their best, to put out the finished CD. And if it is done right, it can be a piece of music that is played over and over, eventually becoming classic rock.

Listen to Eric Clapton's "Layla." Electric or acoustic, it doesn't matter. It is a quality piece of work. Bad records don't last. They just don't hold up to the test of time. Make sure that all you do is quality. Deliver a quality product or service, be a quality person, and demonstrate quality leadership. Quality translates into long lasting classic rock.

I knew my life as a rock and roll disc jockey was going to have a short shelf life. Not only was I going to have to work hard and strike fast, but I had to be the best there was in all I did. The segues between songs had to be perfect, whatever I said before or after a song had to be correct, entertaining, and timed just right, and the whole show had to be smooth and flow without interruption. The audience might not talk about how perfect my show was, but they were going to point it out, if it sucked, by not listening.

★ Satisfaction

Cris, my stepson, told me over dinner a few months ago that he had downloaded a "really cool song" from Bon Jovi called "Livin' On A Prayer," and he wondered if I had ever heard of it. With a smile and a very strong dose of cockiness, I told him that in August of 1986, I had been one of the first disc jockeys in the country to play the song when it first came out. Of course, the cockiness went right out the window when he said, "It was *that* long ago?"

Jon Bon Jovi recently released his tenth studio album, and it should have come as no surprise to anyone that it was an excellent piece of work. In fact, it almost immediately went to number one on the charts. Bon Jovi is good, and he and the band are good every time. He takes the time to put out a quality, long lasting product. He has the same band. He has the same wife, his high school sweetheart. I am assuming he has the same kids. This is just a quality, stand-up guy.

Maybe it is something in the New Jersey water because Bruce Springsteen is the same way. Whenever Springsteen

releases a new album, you know it will be good. When
you buy a ticket to see him in concert, you know you will
get what you paid for and more. That is the reputation
you want for your product or your service. And you have
to keep that level of quality at all times. There are no
shortcuts in maintaining a quality reputation. You don't
want to lip synch, just ask Milli Vanilli.

> At KLOL, the entire staff went out of their way to
> make sure things were done right. In the early 1980s,
> Bruce Springsteen was coming to Houston. We decided to
> put billboards around town and a big ad in the newspaper,
> welcoming him and the band. The idea was to re-create
> his most famous album cover, Born To Run, using the
> morning team, Charlie Weiss, and me. It worked. It was
> brilliant and perfect, right down to the tuft of hair that
> sticks out on the back of his head. I am sure we had a
> decent shot in the first hour or so, but we kept at it all
> afternoon until it was perfect. It must have been over one
> hundred degrees in the warehouse studio where we were
> shooting the photos, but our persistence and the quality of
> work we all put into our efforts paid off. I have the picture
> framed in my office. To this day people do a double take
> when they realize it is me and not Bruce.

A successful band does the same in the studio and in
preparing for a tour. They listen to the recordings over
and over to make sure they are perfect. You don't want to
play your favorite band's CD and hear someone sneeze in
the background. Successful bands go for the best, not good

enough. And the good ones keep up that level of quality as they prepare for a tour. If I liked the CD, that's what I want to hear when I pay well over one hundred dollars for a ticket to see the band live.

You can do the same with your product or service. One of the things we did to ensure quality at The Space Store was to test every toy we sold. Those tests consisted of me bringing each item home to see how long it would actually last with a house full of boys.

We wanted to be certain when we shipped something that it was the best it could be, and we could stand behind each and every product. We tried on the flight suits; we watched the DVDs; we ate the space food. We checked it all. And we backed it all up with quality customer service.

Your product or customer service will be remembered long after you are gone, bad or good, so put yourself in your customer's shoes. Whether Converse or Prada, customers are the same. They want a quality product or service, and they want great customer service to back it up. One of the most powerful things you can do is to pose as one of your customers and go through the actual process they experience.

★ Leader of the Pack

Who would have ever thought that Bono, lead singer for U2, would be one of the most widely respected rock stars in the world, not only for his music but for his leadership and work with poor countries and disadvantaged people across the globe. Bono has changed the image of rock stars around the world, or at least some of them. He has taken a leadership role in solving problems around the world. He is not a world leader, and it is not expected of him, but he does it because it is the right thing to do.

Whether you lead the band, own the company, or work the line, you are setting an example for others and can set the tone for everyone around you. As a leader, you have to stand up, take charge, and do what is right, setting a good example for those who follow. And take responsibility for your product.

Billy Squier's career came to a jolting halt after the release of the music video for "Rock Me Tonite." His stunningly bizarre dancing and flopping around in the video sent fans running for the exit doors. The performance, forever immortalized on video, ruined his macho, rocker image, and the fans deserted him, never to return. I was writing a rock newsletter at the time, and Billy originally claimed all credit for choreographing the video. Once the scathing reviews started, he quickly tried to blame his management, explaining that he had nothing to do with the video and was only following their advice and directions. Either way, Billy should have stepped up, taken full responsibility, and said, "Yeah, it was a stupid thing to do. I looked like an idiot." I guarantee he would have gone on from that point and retained his rock star status.

I have never liked to hear a band blame a bad record on their producer. If your name is on the album, step up and take responsibility. It ultimately all goes back to you. No one cares if your producer made the call. It is your product, and your fans expect and deserve the best you can do. If you don't like what the producer, the team, or your co-workers are doing, find a way to make it better. Speak up. Find a solution. Do something instead of assigning blame later. And believe me, fans will accept an apology. They won't accept an excuse. And the same goes for your customers.

★ Welcome to the Jungle

A band is a perfect example of teamwork. When they are playing well together, it is teamwork at its best. A band has to play together. If you have an idea for something different, on stage, in front of an audience is not the time to play a different song or lick on the guitar. You have to work with and respect the rest of the band.

There was a refrigerator at KLOL that seemed to be a magnet for food thieves. Linda, our late night jock, had had enough when her sandwich went missing again one night. The next night she put her sandwich in the refrigerator like she always did and went to do her shift. When she returned an hour later to retrieve the sandwich, this time, she was smugly happy to see it missing. After her shift ended early

*the next morning, she typed a note, taped it to the front of
the refrigerator, and we all read, "To the lowlife who took
my sandwich last night. Hope you enjoyed the food. It was
made with two pieces of Wonder bread, lettuce, tomatoes,
and a can of Kal Kat Tuna Flavored Cat food." No one
stole anyone else's food for a long time after that. We were
a cohesive team!*

I am certainly not suggesting you feed your band cat
food. What I am saying is be a part of the team, and work
together towards your common goal. No successful person
does it alone.

My Dad used to say, "If you're not going to give 100
percent in this family and to anything you do, I'd prefer
you not even do it at all." I believe the language he used
was a little more colorful at the time, but that will do for
now. You get the point. Give 100 percent of your efforts to
your team or your band.

★ R-E-S-P-E-C-T

Classic rock never goes out of style. Rock music from
the '60s and '70s still makes the Top 100 lists each and
every year. It's the same with basic manners. They never
go out of style as well. Whether it is answering all your
fan mail or holding the door for someone, manners always
equal quality.

We are all inundated with e-mails, calls, and text

messages these days. But no matter who you are or how busy you are, you need to return phone calls and e-mails. I know you get a lot, but that's the price you pay for fame. You chose to have a phone and an e-mail account, and you chose to give someone the information. You never know when this small but important common courtesy will lead you in another exciting direction.

Disc jockeys are not very good about answering the request lines. We didn't really take requests since it was a time-consuming and sometimes irritating job. However, I did my best to answer as many calls as possible. It paid off big time one afternoon when Slash from Guns'n'Roses called from his Houston hotel room because he was bored watching cartoons. The band was opening for The Rolling Stones that night at the Houston Astrodome and there was a blackout on interviews. I ended up with an exclusive Slash radio interview because I answered the phone. And since I already had backstage passes as the emcee for the show, Slash extended an invitation to "come by and say hello" when I was backstage. When I walked into his dressing room, I got a big hug like we were old friends. I don't think he realized it, and I don't think anyone else saw it, but when he hugged me, one of his long, black, coarse, wavy hair strands got caught between my two front teeth. That was the weirdest flossing I have ever had. I think of it every time I see him on television or hear him on the radio.

As I was making initial calls for book research, a band publicist in Los Angeles said something that really stuck with me. I was surprised he had called me back and I thanked him for the courtesy. His replied, "People in this business don't return calls because it would mean giving up power." That is just insane, but it is how a lot of people think in rock and roll and in every business. Sometimes, it just truly amazes me that we humans get anything done.

★ Time

Next on our list of classic hits, be on time. By the way, to me that means be there about ten minutes early. When I was on the radio, as spontaneous as it sounded, wild and off the cuff, it wasn't. It was planned down to the second. When an interview showed up late or didn't call when they were supposed to, it could completely disrupt the flow of the show. If you're good, you can cover until you recover, so listeners might not notice, but it would throw me off. And it was just downright disrespectful to an air personality and a radio station that was giving up precious air time to help promote their music.

There were also a few bands that inadvertently taught me what not to do. I had taken prize winners to see Rush in concert, and part of the prize was what we called a meet and greet with the band after the show instead of before the performance. I always dreaded these things when they were planned after the show instead of before the performance.

You knew it was going to be a late night, and I couldn't leave because I was in charge of the contest winners. It was my job to make sure they got to meet their favorite band. Rush took it to new extremes. Although the show ended around ten thirty, it was close to one in the morning when they finally brought us backstage to see the band. I was fit to be tied, as we say in Texas. My winner had to be at work at six in the morning, and the rest of us didn't go in much later. It was just a terribly rude thing to do to the fans and the radio personnel. To top if off, they were not in the least bit personable and barely looked at us or spoke to anyone. They quickly signed autographs, took the obligatory pictures, and left. Would you like to guess how often I played a Rush song or talked about the band after that?

Nothing can get me going like being made to wait. If I have taken the time to give you my business and made an appointment, I expect to be seen on time. If you tell me something will be ready on a certain date, that is when I expect it.

I know that stuff happens and sometimes there is no way to get around being late or not having something ready if circumstances are out of your control. However, you can take the time to let your customer know that you'll be late. Don't make someone wait to do their job because you haven't done yours.

Quality

★ Always give a quality product or service

★ Your quality will define your long-term reputation

★ Take responsibility for your work

★ Set an example as a leader

★ Work as a part of the team

★ Be on time

★ Answer calls and e-mails quickly

★ Basic manners never go out of style

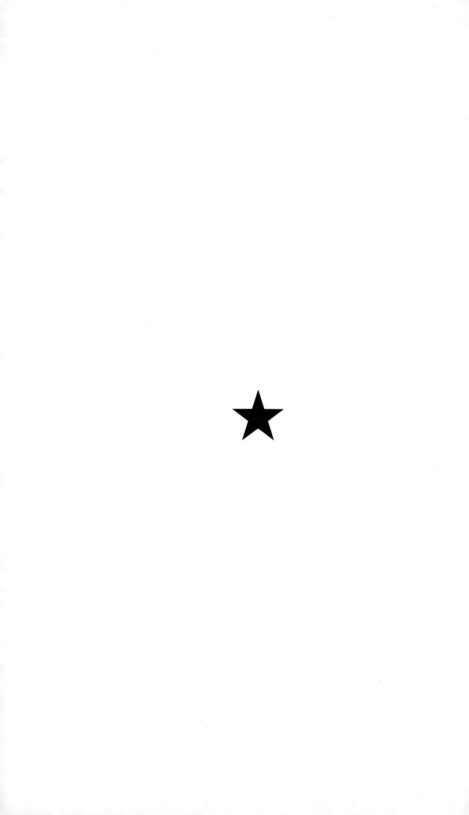

Plan Your Tour:

Organization

★

"Get it together, you can get it all."
Scorpions

A band doesn't play a great show in one city, and then wake up the next morning and say, "So, dude, where ya wanna go next?" There is a plan. It is a rather intensive itinerary that encompasses the entire tour: the city, the venue, the hotel, transportation, interviews, meals, who gets paid what and when, and even more. It is all planned in advance so they can get to as many fans as possible. And that also includes bringing the right amount of merchandise to sell and making sure local stores are stocked with the CD.

Prior to the tour, there has to be even more planning right from the very beginning. You can't call a record company and say, "Hey, we're thinking about recording some kind of music. You interested in us?" Most often, the band picks a name and already has a music genre in mind.

They write some songs and go into a studio to record them. They take some pictures and write a bio. Then and only then do they start to contact record companies about a record deal. And they certainly don't try to get any radio airplay or hit the road for a major tour until there is a product to sell–their CD!

> When Michael Jackson came through Houston on his "Bad" tour, I was witness to some of the most precise tour organization I ever saw and have ever seen since. As a friend of his manager, Frank Dileo, I joined the tour at their downtown Houston hotel and proceeded to the concert venue with the entire entourage. Everything was precisely timed with everyone in predetermined cars and positions. Once at the show, I found myself in the not too common position of being assigned a bodyguard since I was part of their group that night. After the show was over, I was assigned to one of the decoy vans, and off we went with screaming fans in hot pursuit. As if the entire evening hadn't been surreal enough, we then got on the freeway to head back to the hotel. It was then that I noticed the freeway had been shut down in the direction of the hotel for our motorcade. At the time, Michael was just that big. And believe me, that took some planning in advance.

You may not play the guitar or have a world tour planned soon, but you do need to know where you are going and what you will need along the way. You need a written plan of what needs to be done and in what order, and you need a system to keep track of information and appointments, organize finances, maintain a filing system, and make backup plans for the unpredictable. If you get yourself organized and stay organized, you'll be way ahead of the competition.

★ Walk This Way

Most bands don't start out with a business plan in writing. And you don't necessarily need one either. But you do need to know what it is you want and basically how you plan to get there. I am not a fan of big, elaborate business plans that come across like page after page of hot air. You may need one though, if you plan to go looking for large amounts of capital from people you don't know. They will want to know how you plan to spend every dollar they give you.

If the idea is to start your own business or grow the one you have, at least have a plan in your mind of what it is you really want to do and how you are going to get there. It may take some time, but have a plan and start it now. No band agrees to launch a major tour without everything down to the last detail in writing, including payment and technical specifications.

Bands add a list of requirements to their performance contracts. The additional document is called a "rider."

*It specifies technical requirements, dressing room require-
ments, and other needs and details down to the last M&M,
literally. Van Halen used to request bowls of M&M can-
dies with all the brown M&Ms removed.*

*Of course, this story made the rounds whenever some-
one wanted to highlight what prima donnas some rock
stars can be. That actually wasn't the real reason for the
demand. The demand was true, but it was there because
the band knew, more often than not, that if the brown
M&Ms had not been removed then the rider probably had
not been read, and their technical specifications for the
show had not been met. Not only was the show probably
not going to be the best they could do, but it also became
a safety issue with that much power, equipment, and pyrotechnics on the stage. If the band saw one brown M&M,
the entire production had to be checked line-by-line in the
rider. In the middle of the hundreds of technical requirements in that rider, the actual line item read, "There will
be no brown M&Ms in the backstage area, upon pain of
forfeiture of the show, with full compensation." Ouch.*

So, just like a band decides what city to play and what is
needed in each city to make the show happen, you have to
figure out the basic steps you need to take and in what order
to proceed. What's most important? Keep a running list on
your computer that you can edit and change as needed.
Nothing fancy, no charts, just a list that you can refer to
when it is time to take the next step towards success.

Here are some things you need to keep in mind: the name of your company, a one sentence description of what you do, your logo and look, who is your customer, how do you reach them, business cards, a Web site. You can waste a lot of time and money if you run in blind and try to do it all at once. You really need to prioritize. You can't market to customers if you don't have a name and can't describe what it is you do. When I consult with a small business, here is the very basic list I start with:

- What do you want to do?

- What is the name of the company or product?

- Write one sentence that sums up what the company does or what the product is.

- Create a tag line or slogan.

- Design a logo and look, and use a professional.

- Prepare business cards and letterhead, use a professional.

- Create a Web site, and again use a professional.

- Identify and locate your customers.

- Begin your marketing efforts.

- Decide whether you want the brown M&Ms or not!

★ I Still Haven't Found What I'm Looking For

What if you wrote the best song in the world, knew it was great, and would be a multi-million seller? But then you couldn't find it? You have to keep up with information and know where the information can be found. We'll talk about technology a little more in the next chapter, but as a part of being organized and competitive in today's world, you must have a computer and a PDA and/or cell phone.

If you haven't learned to use the calendar function on your cell phone or don't have an electronic organizer, it is time. You can't carry a paper calendar around with you anymore, or a big, bulky organizer. You need something not only with the calendar function but also a device that will sync with the e-mail/address/calendar program you use on your computer such as Microsoft Outlook.

> *Whenever I would head to a show, it was fairly typical backstage operating procedure for no one to have my backstage passes or my tickets or any idea who was supposed to have taken care of it. It never ceased to amaze me and I am sure it hasn't changed much. Many of us, in radio and record promotion, used to joke about how many years of our life were spent waiting for someone to find someone who knew something or had the right list.*
>
> *So, I always tried to make sure I had the name of the person who was supposed to leave the items, their job title, and if at all possible, a phone number. More often than not, it alleviated a lot of problems and got me backstage much more quickly.*

I carried an organizer early on and transferred it all to an electronic PDA as soon as they were available. These days my Treo is with me at all times. Every time I get a business card or write down a name and number on a piece of paper, I later transfer it all to the Treo, and then sync it with my computer.

You should do the same. You never know when you may need that information in the future. Having an electronic organizer with you at all times will save you more time than you can ever imagine. And with today's technology you should be able to put all of this on your phone. It will save you time and money and put you miles ahead of everyone else because you have it and know where it is. Phone numbers, names, e-mails, and addresses will all be at your fingertips.

If you still can't get over your paper addiction, you can carry around a small notebook and pen to make notes when your PDA or computer aren't available. Lots of musicians do this to jot down lyrics if they think of something. I do it when I think of something for the book, an idea for another book, a thank-you note I need to write, lots of things, and then I transfer it to a computer, save it, and sync it once back at the office.

In this world, you can't escape the paper altogether. You will need some sort of filing system. Get a file cabinet and make it a regular habit, either daily or weekly, to file things in an organized manor. I keep a box on top of the file cabinet and file it all away every Friday morning with coffee in hand. It is not one of my favorite activities, but I force myself to do it. I'm grateful later when I need to find something.

★ Back in Black

Okay, you've gotten the big record deal and the record company has given you a nice cash advance. Don't spend it. Don't gamble on whether or not you will have a hit. All this organization is going to give you more time to make money, but keep a handle on it, know where the money is and where it is going.

> Following David Bowie's Glass Spider World Tour show in Houston, I joined Bowie and Peter Frampton, lead guitarist on this leg of the tour, for drinks at a local luxury hotel. In 1976, Frampton had released Frampton Comes Alive, an album that went on to become the biggest selling live album in rock music history at the time. By the end of 1976, Peter had earned millions of dollars in concert fees and royalties. An amazing guitarist and charming person, Frampton related the story of how managers and handlers went through most of the money because he wasn't paying any attention. He learned from that experience to keep an eye on the money, and said, "No one can watch your money better than you."

This should be a given in this section, but I'll remind you anyway. Pay your bills. You don't want the drum company to come on stage during the show and take the drums back. Keep up with payments and, even better, try not to have any payments. Used equipment and a smaller van are just as good as brand new stuff and a tour bus when you are starting out.

Get any agreements that involve money in writing. As much as I appreciate integrity and a handshake, I still want it in writing. Bands have it in writing before they play a note on that stage. It's in writing before they even head to that city.

Last but not least, when it comes to money matters, make sure anything going out requires your signature or approval. No matter how wealthy you become, always sign the checks yourself. Don't give anyone the power to sign for you.

★ Livin' on a Prayer

When your tour bus breaks down on the way to the next gig, it should be no problem. You have your extensive itinerary with you, you know where it is, and you also have important phone numbers and contacts in your PDA right there in your pocket. You know who to call to get things done or fixed. Being organized is going to help you when things don't go exactly as planned. You'll be able to stay calm, go with the flow, and maneuver the bumps in the road.

My rock radio show at KLOL was planned out to the second each and every day before I went on the air. I would go through the music scheduled for my show and

have all the CDs stacked in order together with the com-
mercials and any promotional cards I needed to read.
I also put together a plan, a show sheet, where I wrote
down what I was going to talk about each time I turned
on the microphone. It was a very precise plan and done in
advance of the show. That way, if anything was missing,
I had plenty of time to get it taken care of or replaced.
All that wild and crazy rock and roll "spontaneity" was
actually a couple of hours of planning ahead.

Life has curves and plenty of them. It is unpredictable, and there will never be anything you can do about that. Kids, school, loved ones, business, health, or something will always change. Be willing to go with the flow but be organized all the same. When your guitar string breaks onstage in front of fifty thousand people, you'll know where to find the extra strings and can keep the show going.

Organization

★ Saves you time

★ Keeps you on time

★ Puts you ahead of others

★ Makes you more money

★ Keeps up with the money you have

★ Reduces stress

★ Helps you manage the unexpected

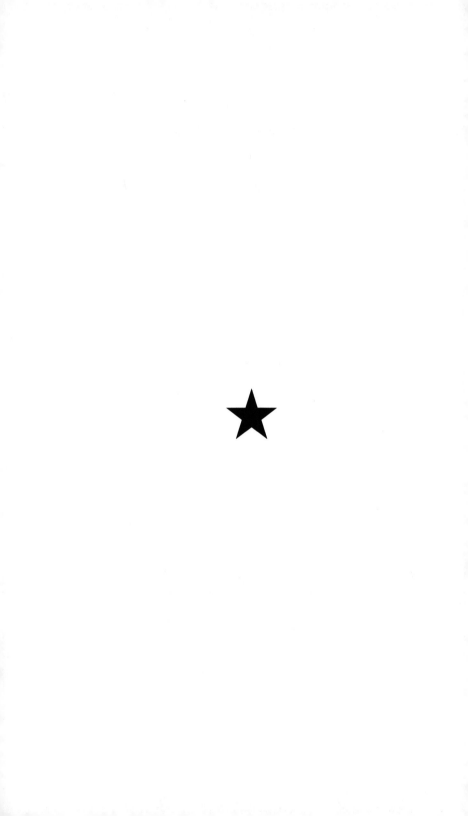

No One Will Ever Pay to Download Music:

Technology

★

"Fear, fear, fear. Of a new thing."
Bon Jovi

It would be a pretty boring rock show without technology. Technology fuels the lighting, the sound, the pyrotechnics, the must-have fog machine, and just about everything else you see on that stage except the performer, though sometimes it's hard to tell if they are animatronic or human. Either way, it is technology that keeps it all running and makes it more entertaining.

The superstars that have embraced new technologies continue to succeed. Genesis, a band that has always been at the forefront of new performance technologies, was the first to use a system developed by Vari-Lite, a lighting system that made their already spectacular show even better. While most of the industry took a "wait and see" attitude towards Steve Jobs and his crazy iTunes and iPod ideas in their early stages, U2 and Bob Dylan jumped on board and sold millions more tracks.

What about you? Have you embraced new technology, or are you still transferring your favorite albums onto cassettes for your car? Sounds pretty antiquated, but some people refuse to move on and accept new technology. Googling yourself, writing a blog, creating a podcast, loading music onto your iPod should all be phrases that make sense to you. If not, it's time to wrap your arms around all the new technologies in the recording studio of life and business.

You'll need a Web presence for your products or service, and e-mail is a must. Not only must you have an e-mail address, but you must also use it and check it on a regular basis. Nothing gets me crazier than a person who gives me their e-mail, and then says a few weeks later, "Oh yeah, I did give you my e-mail. But I rarely check it."

I was always so entertained by a band that gave me my money's worth; a band or performer that utilized all their talents and everything technology had to offer, even if I wasn't paying most of the time. Now you need to be willing to do the same, to learn and move forward with technology. If you can't, find a fifteen-year-old down the street to do it for you. Keeping up with technology will keep you ahead of the competition. You'll be able to use it to organize, create, network, and promote yourself or your product so much more effectively.

★ My Generation

It's kind of hard to put on a good rock show without the proper equipment. Without a guitar, amp, and sound system, nobody is going to hear the music. Whether it's a large-scale stadium show or a small club gig, a band has to have the proper equipment in order to bring their product to the fans. The more up-to-date the equipment is, the better chance the band has of putting on a decent show.

I touched on this subject briefly in the chapter on organization, but I'll elaborate more here. You are going to need the proper equipment as well. Just to start with the basics, you'll need a computer, preferably a laptop, and you'll need a phone that doubles as a personal digital assistant (PDA), such as a Treo or iPhone. It needs to be something that will synchronize with the address and calendar application you use on your computer.

This new technology is going to keep you on top of your game. And everybody else's. Now someone right here is undoubtedly going to reply to my advice with some smarty pants retort, like saying, "Stephen King, the best-selling author, doesn't have a cell phone." Well, you know what? Stephen King is a multi-millionaire writer, so he doesn't need a cell phone because he has people with cell phones. Plus, he likes AC/DC, and that makes him okay in my book.

Melissa Etheridge is a personal favorite of mine. As one of the first major-market radio stations to embrace

Melissa, I had a professional friendship with her. She always made it a point to call or drop by my show for lengthy interviews prior to concerts or album releases. She also has a wicked sense of humor.

The first time Melissa spent some time with me on the air was around the time that fax machines were becoming all the rage in business. The day after Melissa's Houston show, I started to get calls on the private backline into the studio from strangers. Each said the same thing, "Melissa said to call you and say hello." Apparently, she had given out my name and number on stage in San Antonio and encouraged the entire audience to call. I thanked them all for taking the time to call long distance, and then I told my listeners how thoughtful that was and mentioned they should fax Melissa a thank you note to her home fax machine. This was also around the time fax paper came in one long, inconvenient roll. Melissa called a few weeks later when she got off the road and suggested a truce. She had an entire roll of fax paper unwound all over her home office.

CDs just about gave me heart failure when they were first introduced to radio stations. I knew how to cue up a record perfectly so that it started just right on the air. Of course, if it was scratched and skipped, that was another thing. CD's did sound better and rarely skipped. I finally gave up my vinyl records and embraced the new technology, although I did keep a wary eye on those little things for awhile.

Other new technologies have found their way into radio stations these days as well. There are rarely records or even CDs. Now everything is on a computer with touch screen access. And a lot of the time, the disc jockey is not even there. It's all been pre-recorded and dropped in between songs. If radio stations sometimes sound automated and impersonal these days, it is because they are.

If your VCR is flashing the time, you really need help. First of all, we have to get rid of the VCR so we can start to let your inner geek shine. I am a regular geek girl these days with my Treo phone/PDA, laptop, and iPod. I am sure within a few years it will all be in one device the size of my little toe, and I will sit down and tackle yet one more instruction manual. You can do it, too. We'll do it together.

★ Video Killed the Radio Star

It used to be that you recorded an album and went on tour. You did a few radio interviews, and, if you were lucky, you did a television show or two. MTV changed all of that. If you didn't have a video to go along with the song, you weren't getting any airplay.

Now, not only does a band have to have a video that goes along with the song that looks like a mini-movie production (and costs like one too), they also have to update their equipment on a regular basis, use new technologies in the studio, make their music available on iTunes, maintain a bitchin' disco Web site, write a regular blog, and create a weekly video podcast. And if that's not enough, they also need to post goofy stuff from backstage or the tour bus on YouTube and update their MySpace page.

> *Technology has even invaded rehearsals, and I'm addicted to it. Rehearsals.com puts you right into the rehearsal studio to watch the greatest recording artists prepare for concerts, television appearances, tours, and recording sessions. Imagine having a band rehearse in your own living room. This is about as close as you can get. Tommy Nast, one of the principals with Rehearsals.com, was a rock star in his own right during my radio years as the force behind Album Network, one of the leading music industry trade papers at the time. He continues to succeed at what he does because he continues to utilize the latest in technological advances in the entertainment industry to find more ways to bring more entertainment to more people.*

I was told to stop giving out my e-mail on the air, that it would never catch on, and that we didn't need a Web site at KLOL. These days, children are born with their own Web site. Okay. Maybe not all of them are, but you get the point. You are going to have to communicate and function the way others do if you want to succeed in business. If you want to live in a cabin in the woods and be left alone, then you don't have to have e-mail.

I know it can all be daunting, but take one thing at a time, educate yourself, and learn what is out there and how to use it for your business. If everyone is talking about YouTube or podcasting, find out what it is, and find a way to use it for your business.

For example, go to the iTunes site at www.apple.com, and on the podcasts page, type in a competitor's name or a like product or service. Chances are there is an audio or video podcast, or hundreds of them. Watch what others are doing, and then run with the idea.

One of the greatest things about all this technology is that no matter where you are or what you are doing, it is all working on your behalf 24/7. You could be home in your pajamas, but if you use the technology available, no one has to know where you are or how big (or small) your company is.

You can be on the golf course, in a boat, anywhere in the world. There was a cartoon we used to keep on the bulletin board at the Space Store because people always thought we were actually much bigger than we really were. Only three of us ran a company that shipped almost a million dollars worth of merchandise each year. The cartoon depicts a large dog sitting in a chair working on a computer with a little dog at her feet. The big dog says to the little dog, "No one knows you are a dog on the internet." Come to think of it, Amazon.com could still be in Jeff Bezos' garage, albeit a much larger garage than he started with.

★ Beast of Burden

Imagine you are at a concert you have waited months to see. You are there watching your favorite band of all time, and right in the middle of your favorite song, the lead singer stops to check his BlackBerry and text someone. Technology has a good side, but it has its evil side as well.

Just because you have all these cool little gadgets doesn't mean you have to use them all the time. There is a time and a place for it all, and it's not when you are supposed to be giving someone your attention or when it will disturb others around you.

> *I am not sure how I would have handled it if a band had insisted on answering their cell phone, texting someone, or checking their e-mail while I was trying to interview them live on the radio. In 1985, it wasn't an issue. I can tell you that when I would interview bands backstage or at another public venue, it was very irritating if they insisted on looking around to see who was there or who was noticing them. Odds are, I didn't interview them again anytime soon. It was disrespectful to me and boring to my audience. See ya!*

The same goes for you, whether you are in a meeting or at your kid's play. Turn the gadgets off and pay attention to what is going on around you. We really did get by without cell phones and BlackBerrys for a long time. It can still be done.

And if you must take that call, watch your volume and

your subject. No one really cares about your toe fungus at your job or anywhere else for that matter. There are just some things I don't want to overhear at a rock show, movie, or in the office. And there are definitely some things I don't need to know about your body parts or your love life. Even though it is a personal phone call, it doesn't mean we can't hear you.

Just as your mother always had that one last warning before you went out the door to have a good time, I have one for you as well. Learn the new technologies, but learn their downsides as well. If you absolutely must create a personal page on MySpace or Facebook, be careful what you write.

Even if you cancel the account or forget about the page and don't touch it for years, anything you have written will be floating around out there in cyberspace for years to come. It can be found by the recruiter who was just getting ready to offer you a great position with the company that you have always wanted to work with at a salary that made your eyes bulge. If they find what you wrote in college about your preference for smoking marijuana naked in public parks, the amazing job could vanish into thin air. Pay close attention. What you write and post on the Internet today can be read later by colleagues and future employers.

Last but not least, Google yourself occasionally and find out what others have to say about you or your product. Simply go to www.google.com and type in your name or the name of your business or product and see what comes up. It's a great way to keep up with public opinion, and it also keeps the not-so-pleasant surprises, such as a bad review, to a minimum. You can't stop the bad reviews, but you'll know fast if there is a problem and can fix it before any more comments hit cyberspace.

★ Simple Man

At the 1989 MTV Video Music Awards Jon Bon Jovi and Richie Sambora performed two of their most recent hits, "Wanted Dead or Alive" and "Livin' On A Prayer," on acoustic guitars. No band, no pyro effects, no screeching electric guitars. They were just two musicians and two acoustic guitars. That performance is credited to this day with giving birth to the extremely popular *MTV Unplugged* series.

I use that story to highlight the fact that sometimes technology can be put aside successfully. Technology can also overshadow what you are trying to do. Imagine how good a rock show would be if all the lyrics and everything they said between songs was on a PowerPoint presentation behind the band.

That is what some people insist on doing in presentations, seminars, and other business functions. Every word they say is listed in their PowerPoint presentation. The audience is watching the PowerPoint and not the performer. Eventually they go into that zombie state, the "I wish this speech would end now," mode.

Okay. This will be the most risqué story in the book. It is not that kind of book and some of those stories will never see the light of day, but my former agent always loved this one so much, I had to find somewhere to put it in the book.

I was at a beautiful luxury hotel in Dallas, Texas, traveling with Ed Leffler and Van Halen. After the show and post-show party, I was tired and went to my room to get some sleep. It must have been about three or four in the morning when the phone rang. It was the hotel manager on duty, calling to let me know that there was a naked woman in the lobby claiming to be Mrs. Leffler, and he wanted to know what would I like him to do about it. He knew I was a friend of Ed's and staying there on the management company's dime, but I was by no means a part of the "official band entourage" or listed as such in the tour itinerary. To this day, I've never been sure why he called my room not the tour manager. I simply suggested he give her one of their nice, fluffy, complimentary bathrobes while I made a few calls to try and find someone "official" to deal with her. Ed, by the way, was not married at the time and was sound asleep in his room with the phone on "Do Not Disturb."

I wish I could tell you there is a formula for all of this, but there isn't. Ultimately, the decision is yours. You'll have to follow your gut and decide what works when for you. To e-mail or to call? Treo or BlackBerry? IM or text? Acoustic or electric? MySpace or Facebook? PowerPoint or your sparkling personality? Bathrobe or no bathrobe? All you have to do is remember that sometimes, simpler is better.

Technology

★ Get a computer and a cell phone

★ Get e-mail and check it, use it, and manage it

★ Become friendly with the Internet and what
it has to offer

★ Google yourself

★ Embrace and learn new technologies

★ Sometimes simple is better

Keep the Makeup On:
Branding

★

"What's your name?"

Lynyrd Skynyrd

What's the name of your band? What kind of music do you play? What's your image? Where are you going to play? How will you promote the band? Which record company should you sign with? Which radio stations play your brand of music? Have you contacted the local newspaper? Are you proud of your music?

Those questions should give you an idea that it takes some work to develop a lasting and memorable brand. We can't all be so lucky as to have The Rolling Stones' tongue. KISS is already wearing the makeup. However, both those bands, as well as many others, worked long and hard to create those brands, promote them, and protect them.

I asked questions about "your band" at the beginning of this section. Now let's translate that into regular business speak. What is the name of your service or product?

Can you explain what you do in one sentence? What is the image you want to convey? Who are your customers? How do you reach them? And last, but not least, can you proudly protect and stand behind that brand? This is an ongoing process for any business and a surefire way to create something people will remember.

This is probably the hardest chapter for me to write because it is my favorite part of doing business. It's like putting together a puzzle with thousands of pieces and the satisfaction you get when you pop in that last piece. This is also the part that makes a lot of people give up and quit. It's hard work and can seem fruitless at times, but then the press calls or sales double, and you are on top of your game again, ready to keep going.

★ Call Me

ZZ Top. Lynyrd Skynyrd. Aerosmith. The Rolling Stones. Led Zeppelin. All are great names backed up with great product and phenomenal branding. For every great band, there are hundreds of other bands with great names but no product or branding to back it up. In other words, they sucked. Or they sucked at marketing.

Let's assume you have a fabulous product or service, and you are going to market it like no one has ever marketed it before. First, you still have to have a name and be able to tell people what it is you do without a dissertation.

Sometimes the hardest part is starting at the beginning.

We get so excited about our new business that sometimes we jump ahead and forget to start with, well, the beginning. I was recently consulting with a client who wanted to jump ahead to marketing ideas. I had to slow him down and back him up. What is the name of your company, and what do you do? You need to be able to discuss who you are and what you do in one sentence—a sentence that is so compelling, people will want to know more. Then, and only then, can you elaborate more.

> *Frank Beard, the drummer for ZZ Top, and the only one without a beard, is responsible for the most lasting name in my family, my mother's nickname. She so reminded her friends of the waitress character on* Alice, *a hit television show at the time, that a few took to calling her by the waitress' name. Frank and Debbie, his wife, were neighbors of my parents, and once Frank picked up on the nickname, he never called her another thing. I'm not even sure he remembered her real name. Soon other neighbors started to call her by her nickname, as well as friends, family members, and my KLOL co-workers. With her signature poofy hair and Texas accent, the "brand" was set. Fran Nicholson was forever branded as Flo.*

Once you have a name, it will make it easier to come up with that short description of what it is you do. From there, you can start to build on that foundation. You really will be tempted to jump ahead, but slow down and make it a strong foundation. With the name and a compelling description, the rest will fall into place a lot easier. It's still going to take work on your part, but it's easier to build the second floor when you have the first floor in place.

★ You've Got the Look

Ask anyone what the logo is for The Rolling Stones and, chances are, 99.9 percent of them will know the correct answer. They probably can't tell you who the Secretary of State is, but they can tell you that Mick and the boys use a red tongue on t-shirts, album covers, and more. Maybe if Condoleezza Rice joined a band or got a cool logo, it would help identify her as Secretary of State.

KLOL, Houston's Rock and Roll Authority. The name and the description were all in one neat little package, and then we added the Runaway Radio, a memorable logo. We proceeded to put it on everything: letterhead, stickers, t-shirts. You name it, and KLOL branded it. There were a few years where you just weren't cool in Houston if you didn't have a KLOL Runaway Radio sticker on the back of your car. I have a picture of Stevie Ray Vaughan, sitting on the back of his pickup truck and posing for a picture for a local music photographer. If you look very closely, there is a KLOL bumper sticker on the back of Stevie Ray's truck. Even at one point, local law enforcement targeted cars specifically with KLOL bumper stickers to be pulled over. Talk about stereotyping.

The point is, when you saw the Runaway Radio, you knew it must be rock and roll. A picture is worth a thousand customers, and the first time someone sees your logo, letterhead, packaging, or anything, that is when they form a lasting impression of you or your product. So, make sure it's a good one.

Also make sure you are consistent with all you do, from your business cards to your Web site to all your materials. This includes the way you dress, the way you speak, the words you choose, the people you are with, and the places you go. It all defines who you are and how people think about you and your product

If you are a woman wearing low-cut, revealing outfits to work, chances are you are not going to be promoted much higher in the company. At KLOL, I found myself branded as "Houston's First Lady of Radio," and I had to find a line somewhere between class and vamp. I also came with my own theme song. Starting with the first KLOL Rock and Roll Auction, someone decided to always play Jimi Hendrix's "Foxy Lady" when I walked on stage or into an event. It perpetuated the brand, but it embarrassed the heck out of me. I still cringe when I hear that song, even in the privacy of my own car.

Whatever image, look, or logo you decide on, stick with it and be consistent so that it is branded into the memory of your customers forever. KISS came into our lives with makeup on, and they used the same makeup design each and every night. When they took the makeup off, consistency was lost, and fans were disappointed. The makeup went back on and the brand survived. It survived to the point that there are now thousands of KISS-branded products including: KISS wine, a KISS coffin (for those lifelong fans), and even a KISS coffeehouse in Myrtle Beach, Florida.

★ You Really Got Me

If you play classical flute and book a gig at an after hours rock bar, chances are the crowd will not be happy. Not happy at all. If you play rock music, find your rock fans. If you play classical music, find the classical music fans. You get the point. Know who your audience is and where they are.

> For most of my rock radio career, I was doing the mid-day shift at KLOL. I wanted to create an identity for my listeners like the morning show's "Groove Dawgs." I saw what the branding did for the guys in the morning, and I didn't see any reason I couldn't do it in middays. We thought long and hard, and we tried to come up with the most common characteristics of my listeners. It all came down to one common denominator. The majority were listening to me at work. I must give credit where credit is due. Christina Ayo, my best friend since we were twelve, came up with the name for my listeners: Steeleworkers. I am still surprised after a speech when a successful, well

dressed business person walks up to me, holds out a hand, and proudly proclaims, "I'm a Steeleworker." Christina's name and the branding continue to this day.

Think about your product. Write down a list of who will buy it. Make a list of where you think these people go, what they watch and listen to, what they read, and the groups they tend to associate with. After this research, you'll have a better idea of where to advertise, what events to attend, and much more. Once you identify your customer, then it's simply a matter of getting their attention.

★ Magical Mystery Tour

Woodstock. Lollapalooza. Willie Nelson's Fourth of July Picnic. All these are great concert events and branding that is forever in our memories. Concerts are an excellent way for bands to promote their product. A lot of bands actually lose money initially in production and travel costs on the road, but they have to get out there and do the shows to reach their audience. Imagine being asked to open for Def Leppard. It is a branding opportunity a rock band can't pass up.

Radio stations probably take advantage of event branding more than any other business. Their station vehicles, plastered with the station logo, call letters, and frequency are parked outside like-formatted concerts with handouts for fans as they go into the show. KLOL always took event branding to the next level. Sure, we did the concerts and venues, but we also created the first Rock and Roll Auction for charity with one-of-a-kind rock items and rock star auctioneers.

Pregnancy seems to be cool and hip now, but when I became pregnant with my first child, there was some concern about my rocker chick image. How was I going to maintain my "brand"? It was suggested on several occasions that I not mention the pregnancy on air and possibly even hide it as long as I could. Demure and quiet however are not two of my strong points so, at seven months pregnant, I posed nude ala Demi Moore for the cover of Houston Health & Fitness magazine. Now keep in mind, I had thrown up for six months and only gained fourteen pounds, starting at 105, so posing nude was not a problem. I was happy to show off my body and brand my pregnancy as a cool, hip publicity stunt. It remained that way until the first labor pain.

Keep up with events in your area that would give you an opportunity to brand your product or service even more, or create your own event. At the Space Store, we would occasionally invite retired astronauts to come in on a Saturday afternoon and sign autographs. Our customers loved getting to meet an astronaut and it branded us as space experts. You could actually *meet an astronaut* at the Space Store.

Again, identify who your customers are, what they like, and where they go. If you have a cool new toy for kids and the Children's Festival is coming to town, you need to be there. If you can't afford a booth, you can still be there. Take some toys and give them away. If the kids like them and play with them, believe me, other kids will notice and parents will start asking where more are available.

I do believe one of my favorite KLOL branding events was the giant bra the promotions department had hung from a billboard touting, "A couple of boobs in the morning." As the sun came up over I-10 in Houston, it became quite apparent that a billboard-size bra was swaying in the morning breeze. It brought out fans, protesters, police, city authorities, and every television station in town.

★ Givin' the Dog a Bone

Rock stars and bands never arrive at a radio station without CDs, t-shirts, and other "swag" to give away. It's all in an effort to brand themselves into the memory of the radio station personnel and eventually onto the play-list of the radio station. At events, they happily sign autographs and occasionally still have photographs to sign.

KLOL had stickers and t-shirts to give away at events and appearances. The morning team had their "Wrap That Rascal" condom key chains, and I had "From the Desk of a Steeleworker" notepads. I never went anywhere without business cards and pictures to autograph.

Spinal Tap, the fictional band, did everything as if they were a real band to promote the movie, This Is

Spinal Tap, *a hysterical parody documentary of the trials and tribulations of a famous rock band. My hands-down favorite rock star giveaway was the colander I received from Spinal Tap. Playing off the parody of the movie, it came with a disclaimer that explained there had been a problem with communication within their organization and that it was actually supposed to be a calendar. I still use it in the kitchen, and it still makes me laugh each time.*

When it came time to promote the Space Store, I knew we had to come up with something just as worthy of branding history. Plus, if I was going to spend my hard earned money on something free for my customers, it had to be something that would make them think of us anytime they needed anything space related. It also had to be something that would catch the attention of others. So we imprinted our name on the infamous Fisher Space Pens, sometime referred to as "the Seinfeld pen." It was much more memorable, and useful, than a business card.

Customers love free stuff. Everybody loves free stuff. Just make sure it works for you and serves its purpose to strengthen your brand and continue to bring in new customers. Put some thought into those items you leave behind. I'm still surprised when someone hands me one of those small, paper yearly calendars. Who uses these? They go in the trash. Give them something they want. I've noticed more conferences putting memory sticks in the take-away bags. Great idea. I can always use one of those. And it's a fantastic way to share information at the conference.

Remember. It's most important to never leave the house or office without checking to make sure you have business cards. If you have a card, you look legitimate, and it gives you something to leave behind, or you have something to write notes on if needed. Just don't be a business-card psycho, which is kind of like a flasher, but who instead pulls out a business card. Scares me every time.

★ More Than a Feeling

Rock stars like Mick Jagger and Sting have a bevy of high priced attorneys, managers, accountants, and advisors to protect their interests and their brand. You may not have quite that many people on the payroll, but you can still protect your own brand.

Okay. I'm guilty. But I learned from my mistakes. KLOL did a billboard when I returned from Los Angeles. The concept was "the music is back." It was to herald my return and be a subtle jab at the disc jockey who was leaving and had been notorious for talking instead of playing music. They dressed me up in a sequin dress, poofed my hair, and put a thick layer of makeup on my face. I hated it. I loved the slogan, but the rest of it was awful. I was so uncomfortable doing that photo shoot and was just as uncomfortable each time I drove past any of the billboards. They were everywhere. It wasn't rock and roll. And you know what? The way the show was put together wasn't that great either. But I didn't speak up and I didn't find a solution. I just went along with it all and hated every minute of it. I know the billboard wasn't the reason the show didn't last, but it certainly didn't help.

If your gut tells you something is not right, it probably isn't. Protect your brand. Don't let anyone talk you into anything that doesn't seem right for your product or service. And no matter how well they package something or present it, ultimately you know if it is right for you and your product.

Never be afraid to protect your brand.

Branding

★ A name says it all

★ A one sentence description

★ Identify your audience

★ Locate and reach out to your customers

★ Give'em something

★ Protect that brand

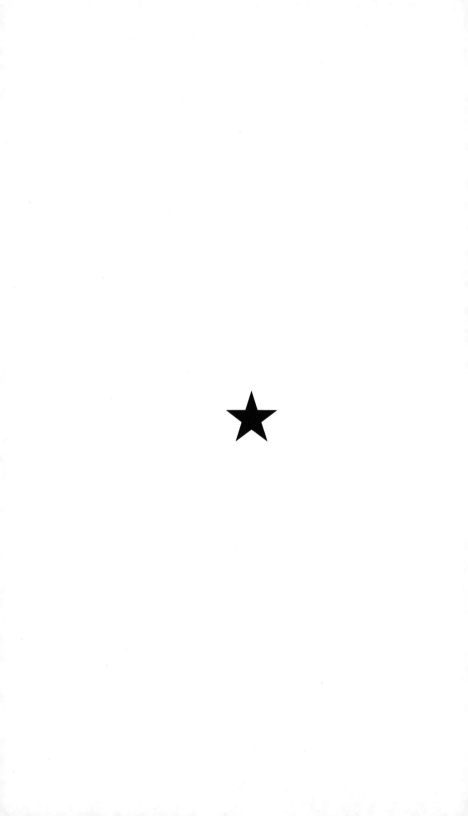

I'm With the Band:

Networking

★

"You're the flame that feeds my fire."
Joan Jett

B ands have record company representatives, disc jockeys, radio programmers, fans, music critics, and management personnel surrounding them with support and
encouragement. If they are doing it right, and the bigger
bands and rock stars are, they are constantly in touch with
these people, promoting their current or next project.
They call it schmoozing. You and I call it networking.

Whatever you call it, it means getting out there and
spreading the word about your business, shaking hands,
talking about what you do, and showcasing your product to
as many people as you can. Remember, most people do not
read minds. They don't know what you do or why you do it.
You have to tell them. You have to tell them how good it
is. You have to tell them to buy it. No one can get the word
out better about your business than you.

Just like a band has all the people mentioned before, you have just as many. The bottom line is that business is all about relationships, and you have to let everyone know you have a hit on your hands, starting with friends, family, and business associates. It all comes down to who you know and how well you work that network of contacts.

There are others ways to network as well. Find a mentor, get out and speak to groups and gatherings, and attend events where you'll meet other like-minded business associates who can help spread the word about you. Any winning team is not only made up of co-workers, but also of supporters and promoters who can talk to others about your business.

You really are surrounded by a large network of people who can help you and will want to help you. It is just a matter of getting the word out, utilizing all of these methods. It takes some time, but that's why they call it work. Best of all, with a large network of friends, family, and business associates, you'll always be in business.

★ With or Without You

Almost every band has started by selling their first recordings and their first concert tickets to family and friends. At first, it's the best way to fill seats and start to spread the word about your show and music.

Now is not the time to be shy about what you are doing. You have to get the word out, and, for the most part, we all have family and friends in some form or another. That's what friends and family are for. They support you and what you do, sometimes, no matter how crazy the idea. Best of all, friends and family have other friends and family, and pretty soon the word is getting out.

> *Legendary drummer Carmine Appice and I became good friends during his stint as drummer for King Kobra. Carmine had played with the likes of Vanilla Fudge and Rod Stewart, and he was on the road at the time of this story with bat-eating Ozzy Osbourne. Carmine had asked to borrow my car to run some errands, and since I was doing a night-radio stint at the time, it didn't seem to be a problem. He would drop me off at the radio station, go do the gig, pick me up after my shift, and I would drop him at the band hotel. Well, that was the night Sharon Osbourne decided to fire Carmine as he came off stage. I ended up with Carmine, his drum roadie, and a complete concert drum set in my living room for a few days until arrangements could be made to get Carmine and company back to Los Angeles with all the equipment. That's what friends are for. At least for a few days . . . .*

Friends and family are probably one of the strongest assets you will ever have, and all too often we overlook that fact. They love you, support you, and can also be brutally honest in a way we sometimes need in business. If your friends and family aren't going to get out there and help promote you, then you at least need to ask why. You might actually need to rethink or retool whatever it is you are doing before you spring it on the rest of the world. But once that is done, you are off to a running start.

★ Takin' Care of Business

Who will play your music? Who will sell your music? After friends and family, a band needs to find a manager, an agent, a record company, and a radio station that will play their music. They need a store that will sell it and a spot on iTunes. And they need to get that "buzz" going within the industry.

Getting out and meeting and talking to people in your field or related fields gets the word out about your business. If you haven't let your business contacts know what you are doing, there is nothing to spread and you are left behind while others "network." You have to work at networking all the time. It is a never ending task, but it's one that pays off in the long run time after time.

Business associates have other business associates. One contact might not be able to help but will remember you or your product when talking to another business contact. The more you network, the more word spreads to others about what you are capable of doing. Your reputation starts to grow and the phone starts to ring.

Business associates are also your best line of defense when you hit a snag. Can't get distribution? Need to replace an employee? Can't get something just right? Ask for advice. Most likely, there is someone in your business circle who has experienced the same problem, figured out a way to solve it, and will be happy to pass on the knowledge.

The networking I did constantly in radio and rock and roll paid off all the time. I was scheduled to emcee a KISS concert at the Houston Summit. As was often the case, the backstage pass and ticket that were supposed to be left for me at the back security gate were not there. Security was tight and my contact was nowhere to be found.

As I was waiting for the problem to be resolved, the big, black, imposing band limousines came through the gates and into the backstage parking garage. As the band and their entourage poured out of their transportation and into the back door, Gene Simmons turned and walked towards the security guard and me. If you have seen Gene's fabulous television show, Family Jewels, on A&E, you know he is a big, intimidating guy who is used to getting his way. Without ever saying a word, he walked over, threw his arm around my shoulders, and turned to walk into the venue's backstage door. Security wasn't about to argue with him. Once inside, he turned to me and said," You still won't come to my dressing room, will you?" It was a standing joke between us. "Nope," I said, and then I walked off with a smile to find my elusive backstage pass. He was a good contact to have!

Your business contacts really will go out of their way to help you with your business. Just remember to be appreciative and to repay the favor on a regular basis. One thing I do constantly is to send articles, links, etc. to my contacts when I see or read something that reminds me of them. Whether they ever read it or use it is beside the point. They know I was thinking about them and they in turn remember my business when it is needed.

★ The Message

Don't you like to read about your favorite band? More often than not, their publicist has planted or suggested that story to a reporter. When The Rolling Stones announce a tour, they do it with a huge press conference (with the big tongue behind them), and invite reporters and photographers from all over the world. And what happens? Their tour becomes the lead story on CNN and hits the cover of major newspapers all over the world. They work it like nobody else.

Never, ever underestimate the power of the media: electronic or print. A story about you and your business is so much more powerful than any advertisement. It's a heck of a lot cheaper too. The media needs you, they need stories, they have to fill with something, and it might as well be you. You can network with the press just like you do with the rest of the world.

Coverage is really not that hard to get. It's just a matter of making the media aware of you and your business. That can be done in several ways. And yes, you can do it yourself. You can send a letter of introduction with a press release you created if there is something new to cover, such as a promotion or new product, or you can suggest a story.

Put together a media list: names, addresses, e-mails, press outlets, and phone numbers after collecting as much information as you can get on the media you want to cover you. It can usually be done with one simple call to the press outlet's main number. You would be amazed how much information you can get if you just ask. And don't forget to ask what format they prefer for story suggestions and press releases. Most outlets prefer e-mail these days, including the information in the body of the e-mail rather than as an attachment, unless they have specifically asked for something.

I always recommend sending a letter of introduction about you and your business. Let the media know who you are, what you do, and what qualifies you to speak with authority on this business or subject. Include your name, mobile number, and e-mail address, and then encourage them to call you if they ever need any information on your subject of expertise.

At the Space Store, I sold NASA and space related souvenirs, toys, and t-shirts. I also had a great relationship with the press, local and national. When they couldn't get a quote from anyone at NASA on something, they would inevitably call me for reactions from my customers. I am not a rocket scientist, but I was always happy to give them a quote.

If you read something that you believe should have quoted you or been a story about you, write a note to the reporter, complementing the article and introducing yourself. With the note, you can suggest that they feel free to contact you for a quote on anything similar, or suggest another story they might like to do about you and your product. A lot of times, there is follow-up on a current story and the press may be looking for a fresh perspective. Make it easy for them to find you.

> When I posed nude and pregnant for that local fitness magazine, at first there really wasn't the reaction I had expected from the public or the media. Molly Smyth, a Houston public relations expert, and my self-appointed fairy godmother, waited for just one distribution location to refuse to carry the issue, then called a local television news desk to let them know that someone was actually offended by my pregnancy.
>
> Oh my! All three local network affiliates jumped on the story, the newspaper ran editorials in several columns for days, and the Associated Press news wire picked up the story and it spread across the country. All because Molly made a call and suggested a story to one reporter.

It is just a matter of getting into what people watch and read. Jeff Crilley, Dallas television reporter and author of *Free Publicity*, makes a great point on the media. His point is that very rarely does the daily newspaper have blank pages or the television anchor come on, saying, "Good evening. Nothing happened today. Good night." These days, there is a lot of space to fill in print, on television and radio, in blogs, on Web sites, and so much more. It might as well be about you.

★ Magic Carpet Ride

Not only do bands put on concerts and shows to promote their music and albums, they also have industry events to keep that promotion going within their network: the radio station programmers and music reporters. I attended countless radio and record conventions where artists, music reps, and radio station personnel had a chance to network for days at a time. I always came away from one of those things with a few more contacts, a little more knowledge about the latest new music, and a little more notoriety for Houston's First Lady of Radio.

Business events, gatherings, and conferences within your industry are a must for anyone who wants to get the word out about their business. It is also a time to gauge the need within your industry for you or your product. You may think you know everything there is to know, but believe me; you will always pick up more knowledge and contacts at one of these things. They are never a waste of time if you keep your eyes open and pay attention. If you make just one new contact, it is worth it, I promise.

Rock and roll conventions were usually called parties. Convention is not a very hip word. Tom Petty had a record release "party" for a new album at Universal Studios in the late '80s. This one was a little different in that only a handful of radio programmers from around the country were invited to hear the whole thing, and then we moved to another part of Universal Studios for the big celebration party with more industry folks and radio station winners flown in for the event. Petty, myself, a representative from his record company, and his tour manager were instructed to follow a guide from Universal Studios into a tunnel system. The oh-so-helpful guide pointed the correct way and sent us into a maze of tunnels, doors, twists, and turns. There is a scene in the movie Spinal Tap where the fictional rock band gets lost on their way to the stage. Of course, everyone in our lost group had seen the movie and we were laughing so hard we cried. We eventually found our way to the party, and I came back with a fun, hip story to tell on the air, further adding to the "Dayna hangs with rock stars" image.

Conventions, luncheons, the occasional happy hour are all excellent networking opportunities. Anywhere there are business contacts gathering, you should be there as well. And who can resist a good party? Hum. I mean, uh, convention.

★ Money for Nothing

Bands play free shows for radio stations all the time, especially the newer, unknown bands trying to make their mark in this world. Radio programmers are happy to be able to offer something to their listeners that they might not get somewhere else, and bands have the opportunity to start building a fan base across the country.

You can build a fan base as well. One of the best ways is to offer your services as a free speaker. The "chicken and rice luncheon circuit" is alive and well in this country, and is always in need of a free speaker. Here is your opportunity to strut your stuff in front of yet more business contacts that have business contacts that have business contacts. You get the picture. Just get up there and give them something they can take away and use in their business. They're there, after all, to network and possibly learn something.

If you hands down do not want to be the rock star and get up and speak in front of a group of people, then consider using some of your networking time to get involved with local charities and community organizations. They can always use volunteers and they always need something for their fund raising auctions. The Space Store constantly donated to silent auctions. We would give a toy basket or an astronaut flight suit, anything that grabbed attention, and we tried to do it for each and every request. It put our name and product in front of thousands of people over the years at a fraction of what it would have cost us to advertise to that many people. Not only that, just think of all the good karma we generated.

> *Dozens of rock stars and other celebrities said, "Yes," when asked to be a part of the KLOL Rock and Roll Auction. They usually had an album to promote, a television show coming out, or some other ulterior motive. But who cares? They got what they wanted and we got a great lineup: Steven Tyler, Joan Jett, Joe Walsh, Tommy Shaw, Jack Blades, Gene Simmons, Starship, Paul Shaffer, Vince Neil, Night Ranger, Earl Slick, Mick Fleetwood, Lindsey Buckingham, Julian Lennon, Ann and Nancy Wilson, Steve Howe, Jon Bon Jovi, Richie Sambora, and the list goes on. We paid all expenses, they donated their time, and we all raised a ton of money for charity. A win-win situation all the way around.*

A newsletter and a blog are good ways to round out your "free services." You are passing on valuable information all the while promoting your business. Make sure you have a newsletter sign-up on your Web site and a link to your blog. And don't use either as a blatant advertisement for your business. Give useful advice, pass on some news, then do a soft sell on your product. For a small business on a limited budget, both are useful and productive networking tools.

As I added reporters to my media list, I also included them in my newsletter mailing list. I had many an article written about the Space Store from a new product I introduced in my monthly newsletter. And the weekly blogs I write online for Smart Girls Rock constantly show up in search engines across the world and have garnered media attention as well.

★ Help

You hear about it all the time. A famous singer sees an unknown performer and takes that person under wing, makes introductions, offers to produce their first CD, and before you know it, another rock star has been manufactured. Someone who is already established in the music business can open many more doors that a struggling musician can't begin to do on their own.

In business, there is always someone who is better at what they do than you, has more contacts than you, and can guide you over some of the inevitable bumps. It is egotistical and stupid to think that there is no one who can help you. Never hesitate to ask someone for their advice. It's not unheard of to find that some of the most successful people in this country, of all ages, in all businesses, have a mentor.

The Texxas Jam was not only a yearly legendary concert event with fans in Texas and surrounding states, it was also a must event for bands, record companies, and radio station personnel from across the state and the nation. It was an opportunity to network with the cream of the crop, including: top artist managers, the heads of record companies, and radio programmers who made the decisions on what records got played on the air and how much airplay they actually got.

It was always in the hottest part of the summer and could be miserable. One particularly hot afternoon, I found an old-fashioned popsicle cooler filled with free popsicles for the road crews and staff to keep everyone hydrated. It was also a very comfortable (and cool) place to sit and watch everyone go by.

Ed Leffler, who was managing Sammy Hagar and later went on to manage Van Halen, got a kick watching me tell people the popsicles were actually a dollar. I think he appreciated a budding entrepreneur when he saw one. We became fast friends that afternoon, and he helped guide me through the most successful years of my career. He introduced me to my agent and took me along for the ride to meet some of the most powerful and famous people in the music business. And what a wild ride it was, my friends. My association with Ed took me to a level most midday disc jockeys never see to this day.

A mentor can be one of the most powerful tools you have in business. Hopefully your mentor has already made some of the mistakes you are headed toward and can steer you in the right direction or at least guide you through solutions. Never underestimate the knowledge that comes with experience, especially when someone is offering to share that knowledge with you and take you to the next level of networking.

★ Bridge Over Troubled Water

Lead singer David Lee Roth burned one of the best rock and roll bridges ever as the front man for Van Halen. It has taken twenty-two years, but he is set to hit the road with the band once again. Apparently, the bridge has been repaired or at least patched for now.

I don't care what business or band you are in. It is a small world, and you never know when you will be working with someone again. Not only do you not want to burn bridges, but you always want to be nice, do the right thing, and keep in touch. It all pays off eventually.

> When I left KLOL to move to Los Angeles, I left with style, class, and plenty of notice. I also made sure we both got quite a bit of press out of the departure. When I decided I had had enough in Los Angeles, a series of events left a door wide open for me to return to KLOL. I walked through that open door and right into one of the highest salaries ever paid to a female, midday rock and roll disc jockey. I left on a good note, kept in touch, and made KLOL the first call when I decided to come back. If there had been a problem when I left, believe me, my life would have taken a much different path.

While you are taking care of your bridges, hold on to contact info as well. Hang on to every name and phone number you get. When you get the urge to clean out your contact file, go listen to your favorite Led Zeppelin album until the urge passes. You just never know where and when the urge to network might strike.

Networking

★ Friends and family are your most valuable asset

★ Introduce yourself to like-minded business people

★ There is such a thing as free publicity, and lots of it

★ Go to industry events and conferences

★ Offer free services such as a speech, blog,
or newsletter

★ Find a mentor

★ Don't burn *any* bridges

The Interview:

Knowledge

★

"I wanna know all about you."

Heart

There is nothing better than a great, compelling interview on the radio for the interviewer, the one being interviewed, and the audience. A good interview will go a long way towards more airplay for a band, but a bad or boring interview will probably get you banned from the studio for the rest of your career.

When David Crosby, of Crosby, Stills & Nash, was released from prison in Texas, he moved to a halfway house in Houston. I was fortunate enough to get an exclusive interview with David, and it was the beginning of a lifelong friendship. He wanted to be in the studio. He wanted to talk and play his favorite music. He wanted to tell stories about rock and roll and prison. And he was happy to be back and straight. It was such a mesmerizing interview that I still have people to this day come up to me and say, "Man, I had to pull off the highway and just stop and listen."

You may not be doing radio interviews on a regular basis, but you still talk to business contacts and potential customers daily. You are being interviewed each and every time you talk to anyone. You need to be the person others want to talk to and that special person others seek out at a gathering because you are interesting to be around and can add to any conversation.

Never stop learning and always continue to gather information. Read the paper, watch the news, and pay attention to what's going on around you, not just in your passion but in the world in general. Be a good interview and the business contacts will come to you.

★ Light My Fire

I loved to have any rock star on my show that could spin a good story about anything. David Crosby was one. Sammy Hagar was another. These rock stars truly had a passion for what they were doing, and they enjoyed getting out and talking to their fans. Their knowledge of world events and stories made for great radio, generated more and more fans who in turn would buy their records and concert tickets and also listen to my show. Who wants to listen to someone drone on and on about their album and tour? We know about all that, so now tell us something interesting. A rock star who couldn't talk about anything but his new album was bad for business and ratings.

Know a little bit about everything. Knowledge equals power and power equals more choices, no matter what business you are in. It gives you added depth in making decisions and makes you an interesting person to be around. When I was on the radio, I read everything I could get my hands on: books, newspapers, magazines, the trades, anything. When there was time to fill between records, I always had something to talk about.

It's not that difficult and not that time-consuming to catch a pass of CNN Headline News while you are getting ready in the morning. Check the headlines on your phone, or grab a newspaper and scan the headlines. I guarantee you that you won't be successful in business if you don't know what is going on around you.

> On July 13, 1985, I was rockin' at The Palace Hotel in Philadelphia as a part of the VIP entourage for a history-making event in rock and roll: the original Live Aid concert event. I was surrounded, and completely overwhelmed, by some of the biggest rock stars at the time, including The Rolling Stones, Duran Duran, and many others.
>
> I was on my way to the lobby in the elevator when another obvious attendee joined me. We made elevator small talk. "So you going to the show?" "Yeah." "How 'bout you?" "This is cool." That sort of thing. He went his way, and I headed over to the artist green room in the hotel. An hour later, imagine my surprise when I looked up at a television screen and saw my elevator friend on stage as one of the headliners. That was the only chance I ever had to meet and possibly interview the great Carlos Santana, and I didn't have a clue. Guess I should have read the paper that morning.

It always completely stuns me when I hear someone say, "I just don't have time to catch the news." You know what? You don't have time not to. Sometimes you get but one chance in this world to make your mark. Don't be left in the dark or uninformed!

★ Good Vibrations

It was always evident within the first few seconds if a rock star or band wanted to be doing an interview in my studio. Their body language usually gave it away before they uttered a sound. A grimace on their face, little eye contact, no handshake or embrace. Just a cold fish in the room who was wasting my time and my listeners' time. Not to mention what they were doing to my ratings.

Your physical presence makes a strong first impression anywhere you go. Back when we talked about confidence at the beginning of this book, the same goes here. Stand up straight and walk purposely into a room or up to someone. Look them in the eye with a smile, if appropriate, and then give them a good, firm handshake, not a limp rag or a bone crusher. And remember, in very few situations is an embrace proper. Make absolutely sure before you make that move.

At Michael Jackson's mega concert in Houston for the "Bad" tour, I was taken into the dressing room to meet the superstar right before he went on stage. This was at the height of his stardom, and he was huge. Security and concert personnel were everywhere. The dressing room was almost dark. It was very quiet. The only light came from small pin lights in two photographer's silver umbrellas in the corners. All very surreal. Michael scared me as he quietly came out of the shadows to shake my hand. It was the limpest, clammiest handshake I have ever gotten from anyone. It literally sent shivers down my spine. Every time I see him on television, I feel that handshake. It still makes me shiver.

When you walk into a room, an interview, a gathering, or on stage with your shoulders back and a purpose to your walk, you make an impression as someone who is there to do business. And I'll give you another simple but powerful tool. When you are talking to someone or doing an interview with the press, lean in just a tad. Not enough that you invade their personal space or make them think you're a psycho. Just enough to show that you are interested. It's a trick I even use during conversations and interviews on the telephone. It gives my body the signal to engage.

★ People Get Ready

There were times I played bad records and played them by choice. Almost every single time it was because the artist was a fabulous interview and also treated me like I was a long lost friend. Let's face it. The entertainment business is built on massive egos, and if you stroked mine, you had a better shot at getting on the air. These rock stars knew my name, they knew the station's history, and if I had been around them before, they could recall details from past meetings as if I really meant something to them. These artists had done their homework, or at least their managers had done it for them. That always left a lasting impression.

Anytime you go into a meeting or an interview, you will inevitably come out ahead if you have done some work beforehand. Know who you are meeting with, the subject, the background, and all the facts and figures you can come up with. Whether it is a job interview, a business meeting, or a luncheon, make some effort to do a little homework. It will show, and it will be appreciated and remembered in the long run.

Michael Penn, actor Sean Penn's brother, is a great singer/songwriter. He had a solo effort out and was making the interview rounds. I had seen him a few times on various music shows and knew he was a pretty low-key interview. Soft spoken, quiet, not very gregarious. Not one of my favorite kinds of interviews to do. Plus, after an artist does so many interviews, it can become boring and rote to them.

So, I made some calls until I found someone who could give me a question that would perk Michael up, get his attention, and make for a much more interesting interview. After a few of the standard "how's the tour" and "tell me about the album" questions, I asked Michael how long he planned to keep the old car in his front yard on blocks, and what did the neighbors think about it? He looked at me like I was from another planet, then busted out laughing, and said, "You are good." It made for a much more interesting interview.

I had my radio show planned out well before I went on the air. I knew what I was saying and playing for the next five hours and had it all stacked around me in order. It was completely and totally organized and scripted "spontaneity." Ah, but nothing goes as planned in live entertainment, so when something did go wrong, I was prepared with the next thing and could move on without missing a beat. I knew something was wrong, but the listeners never had a clue.

When you are prepared, you seem genuinely interested in the subject or business at hand. You can think faster on your feet. When crisis does strike, you can start to tap dance and fix it a lot faster than others. All without a customer ever knowing the record skipped.

★ Talk to Me

Nothing was more fun and exciting than doing a live broadcast from backstage at a major rock show. The interviews, however, were challenging. The good ones were with the true rock stars who gave me their undivided attention and really talked to me. The bad ones involved rock stars or wannabe rock stars who spent the entire interview looking around at everyone, checking to see who was looking at them, and flirting with the ever-present groupies.

I come from the old school of radio where I was taught to never say phrases like "all of you." I was trained that no matter how many people are listening, each one has one brain and one set of ears. And in order to make a connection with my listeners, I needed to make each and every one feel like I was talking to him or her and no one else. I still try to do that in meetings and in speeches. It did and does make a powerful connection with individuals in the audience. It's just you and me.

Making a connection with your audience, whether it's a thousand people or one, makes for a lasting impression. And lasting impressions can convert into lasting business relationships. Don't look around. Give each and every person in your audience your undivided attention. Speak directly to them.

★ Listen to the Music

Rock stars are continually looking around to see what other rock stars are doing. In an episode of Gene Simmons's *Family Jewels*, he says, "If a band builds a bigger stage, KISS will build an even bigger stage. If a band sells one million albums, KISS will sell 30 million albums." Successful rock stars and bands pay attention to what's going on around them and to the trends in music, touring, and business.

What good is an interview if you have the greatest questions but don't listen to the answer? Pay attention to what is going on around you. Stop and listen to what others have to say. Not only does it make people feel good to have your attention, you might also pick up some useful information. Everybody has a story and if you just take the time to listen and look around every once in awhile, you'd be amazed what you can gather for future reference.

Dave Mustaine, Megadeth front man, was spouting off on MTV one day about what a waste of taxpayer's money it was to have NASA, our national space program. I was paying attention to what he was saying and it was obvious he had not done his homework. With their tour scheduled to come through Houston, I made arrangements for Dave to tour NASA with shuttle commander Jim Wetherbee and find out about the benefits of space travel to humankind. Dave told me later in the evening that he learned a lot, it was a great tour, but he would definitely pay more attention and learn more in the future before he spouted off about anything, for sure, before I made him go on another field trip.

One of the best real world examples I can give you is a flight attendant on a plane. We've all heard the safety talk hundreds of times. However, I always stop what I am doing, look up at the attendant, and pay attention. It may be information I'll never need to use, but in the event there is a problem, I sure would like to know what I'm doing. And it's a respect thing as well. Again, people like to know that others are paying attention to them no matter what they are saying. Not to mention the extra peanuts you get.

Knowledge

★ Know a little bit about everything

★ Be aware of your body language

★ Be prepared

★ Talk directly to your audience

★ Pay attention and listen

We Can't All Be Keith Richards:

Health

★

"I hope I die before I get old."
The Who

Take a look at Keith Richards, guitarist extraordinaire for The Rolling Stones. Seriously, look at him. How does he do it? One of my favorite jokes is that after the nuclear holocaust, the only things that will be left are cockroaches and Keith Richards.

In 1985, I was seated next to Keith in the VIP room at The Palace Hotel at the original Live Aid concert in Philadelphia. He looked like a corpse then. He's still going strong, and the entire industry stays amazed. How does he do it? Or is his "look" part of the brand he has created?

If rock stars truly lived for just sex, drugs, and rock and roll, most of them would be dead.

It's pretty simple and always has been: eat right, exercise and stretch, spend time with friends and family, play, do things for yourself, and avoid stress. Now, try to do all that while in a different city every day and sleeping on a bus with eight other people who aren't necessarily taking care of themselves, all the while eating most meals in a restaurant or from a convenience store. That is life on the road.

What's the point of creating a million-selling hit record or a successful business if you don't take care of your health and your relationships so that you can enjoy your newfound wealth and fame? Poor health and stress can bring down a business faster than a groupie can get backstage.

★ Soul Food

Many times I ate backstage with the band members, their friends and family, and concert personnel. The food backstage was almost always good with several healthy options to choose from. Bands were very specific about catering needs and made sure their personnel, including performers, management, and crew, were well fed. As with any family, not everyone always ate right but most tried, especially knowing it might be their only decent meal of the day.

> AC/DC can mesmerize an audience for hours at a time, with lead guitarist Angus Young playing his guitar with lightening speed, all the while dressed in a young, English schoolboy's outfit.
>
> Invited backstage after a Houston show, I was asked if I would like to join the band for a post-concert dinner.

While they had been on stage, Young's wife had been cook-ing a full dinner for the band and traveling family members. The band's equipment manifest included road cases that had been custom-fit to her needs, including an oven, stove top, dishes, and cooking utensils. The band always tried to sit down to a full family meal before heading out to meet fans and enjoy the rest of their evening. It was a great way to eat right and stay connected with family. I have been trying to figure out her Pumpkin Soup recipe from that night ever since. It was absolutely delicious.

You know what you need to do, whether you are on tour or not. This is not rocket science. You hear it all the time. I figure you are a fairly smart business person and can pretty much get by with a short paragraph on this subject. Eating right means lean meats with plenty of fruits and vegetables. Sugar and starches slow you down. Anything that comes through a window is probably bad for you.

★ It's a Family Affair

Keeping friends and family close was always a good idea on the road. Rock stars aren't exactly known for their fidelity, and it makes it a lot easier to be faithful with a spouse on the road right at your side. Kids will always keep you in line on the road as well. Nothing keeps you on a schedule like a toddler or two. Frank Beard, drummer for ZZ Top, had twin boys and they were always a fun sight backstage with their matching long hair and mini guitars slung over their shoulders. Last I heard, they are making their parents (still happily married) very proud and are serving our country as United States Marines.

> *Sammy Hagar had not yet joined Van Halen, but he was a huge star in his own right in Texas. He was a wild rocker on stage who could easily captivate 80,000 people at the Texxas Jam each and every performance. During one cross-country tour, Mr. Cabo Wabo pulled up to the Omni Hotel in Houston in his decked-out tour bus with fellow band members in tow. As they disembarked from the cool-looking tour bus, each and every person looked every bit the rock star. But they weren't carrying guitar cases. As I helped the band carry equipment off the bus, bystanders were amused to see it included a high chair, play pen, and stroller, all for Sammy's toddler son. The same son now rocks out with Dad at Cabo Wabo, their tequila bar in Mexico. Hopefully he keeps himself healthy for his kids, just like Daddy Sammy did for him.*

Just about everyone you work with probably has some sort of family even if it is just a group of really close friends. If you need to postpone or reschedule something for a soccer game or a school play, they are going to understand. In fact, most people will be impressed that you have your priorities straight and will think that this is just the kind of person I want to work with. If they are put off by the fact that you need to be with your family, then I can almost guarantee this is not someone you want to do business with. Ever.

★ Start Me Up

Okay. Here is a scary statement. Mick Jagger is a grandfather. Now, with that said, look at your grandfather. Can he run back and forth across a stage, sing, strut, and jump up and down for three hours? No, he probably can't. Rock stars are no different than you and me. They have to exercise and stay in shape to keep up with their business.

I was at a show with headliners Aerosmith. Lead singer Steven Tyler was an acquaintance from events and concerts throughout the straight version of his career. Noticing me in the hall, he motioned me over and asked me to come into his dressing room to help him stretch. Now, I'm sure everyone within hearing distance thought that this was some sort of code for a quickie before the show. It is rock and roll after all. But alas, Steeleworkers, there is no wild Steven Tyler story here. What really happened? I helped him stretch. Look at him. He's a grandfather as well. A very sexy grandfather. And a very limber one.

It is hard work and time-consuming to create a successful enterprise. But it is also hard to spend the money if you are dead. So take a walk. You can do it anywhere, anytime, in any part of the world, in any hotel, on any street. You can make it long, short, around the block, up and down the hotel stairs, or around the conference room. As one very successful company says, "Just do it!"

★ Satisfaction

Rock stars may seem narcissistic to you, but they know that in order to be number one, to be the star, they have to take care of themselves first, physically and mentally. If the lead singer can't go on, the show will probably be cancelled.

You have to do things just for yourself sometimes. *It is okay to put yourself first.* I can't make that any simpler or clearer. Women, especially, tend to take care of everybody and everything before they take care of themselves. What happens, though, is you run out of energy when it becomes your turn.

> *Stevie Ray Vaughan was always such a pleasure to be around. He was talented, he was down to earth, and he was a funny guy, although a little shy. I had not seen Stevie for awhile. His career was taking off, and he was no longer a local Houston musician. He was really making a name for himself all over the world.*
>
> *We were in New York City doing a Grammy Broadcast in the late '80s. The week prior to the annual music awards extravaganza, several radio stations from around the country would all set up in one room, maybe twenty to twenty-five of us. Promoters and managers would parade*

rock stars, television stars, and other celebrities through the room, doing an interview at each table. Stevie had already done several when he caught site of the KLOL logo. He dropped down in a chair with a smile, while I was in a commercial break, and started talking about how well things were going. I had never seen him so happy, so animated, and so dressed up. The guy was actually glowing. He had on a beautiful designer suit and custom cowboy boots. I commented that it must be the suit since I had never seen him quite so dressed up. He looked around, made sure the mic wasn't on, and smiled the biggest smile yet. "I got my teeth capped," he said with obvious pride. "I never knew it would make such a difference in my life."

You need to keep yourself at peak performance so that you can in turn run the business, take care of your employees, and satisfy your customers. And give your employees the opportunity to take care of themselves as well. A facial, a massage, a movie in the middle of the day, or whatever makes you feel good about yourself and keeps you and your business on the right track forward. Remember, sometimes we all need a break from the daily grind.

★ Got Me Under Pressure

Now before I completely ruin the whole rock and roll party image, yes, there were a lot of drugs, much alcohol, and many nights without any sleep. Through it all, the ones that have lasted knew what had to be done. Other than a few rock phenoms like Mick Jagger and Steven Tyler, this business is short-lived. Get in, make the huge amounts of money, and try to stay alive through it all.

Nobody is going to run a successful business or rock band for any length of time when stress, drugs, alcohol, and smoking are regular components of your life. Stress and bad habits can wreak havoc on a business or career.

> Ratt was a huge '80s hair band. Lead guitarist Robbin Crosby had a wild lion's mane of blond hair and stood, what seemed to me, well over six feet tall. He just oozed sex appeal and bad boy image. Robbin was a beautiful man to look at and equally nice to be around. In 1990, I ran into him while I was living in Los Angeles. I was going into a restaurant and he was coming out. Robbin seemed a little rough around the edges, not quite well, but I figured he was just following up a late night with food and caffeine. I was shocked to hear he had developed a bad drug habit and eventually lost everything. On June 6, 2002, Robbin died in Los Angeles of a heroin overdose. It was reported that at the time of his death he weighed almost four hundred pounds.

The bad habits will catch up with you, and stress can manifest itself in many ways, from not being able to sleep to heart attacks and more. For me, I was having horrible dizzy spells on a regular basis because I was grinding my teeth due to stress. And I was a heavy smoker. Now I'll have my glass of wine to relax in the evenings, I quit smoking, and yoga stopped the teeth grinding. Stress and health management should be a part of any business plan, for you and your employees.

★ Play That Funky Music

Golf became a huge pastime for a lot of bands on the road in the late '80s and early '90s. It became common to see a row of golf bags in the luggage hold of a tour bus. These days, it's not unusual to see someone with long hair and wild clothes on a golf course, However, at one point, these guys really stood out.

The rock stars understood that there had to be some fun, a diversion, a way to relax from the normal operations of the day. In fact, fun is becoming a buzzword with a lot of businesses now.

Mötley Crüe was famous not only for their rock music but for their mean game of softball. As they toured the country headlining some of the biggest venues in the nation, they would challenge radio stations to a game in each city. They had uniforms, they had a coach, they had top-of-the-line equipment. This was not just a publicity stunt, but a way to blow off steam and have a little fun with the locals. They took it very seriously. And they usually won.

Studies have shown that organizations that incorporate fun, humor, and laughter in the work environment benefit from less employee turnover, less missed project deadlines, and increased profits. Angela Huffmon, a rock star in the world of corporate training specializing in fun in the workplace, says, "When employees have more fun at work they exhibit higher productivity, offer improved customer service, have better morale, and show increased creativity, less absenteeism, and reduced stress levels." Makes it kind of hard for a business to argue with fun, doesn't it?

Knowledge

★ Eat right

★ Keep family and friends close

★ Exercise regularly

★ Take care of yourself first

★ Avoid the things you know are bad for you

★ Play and have fun

Thank You, Thank You Very Much:
Appreciation

★

"You didn't have to love me like you did,
But you did, but you did. And I thank you."

ZZ Top

Rock stars can be so self-absorbed that showing appreciation to others isn't exactly at the top of their set list. The smart rock stars realize that no one does it alone, and those are the ones that say thank you with everything from gold and platinum albums and an exclusive interview to premium concert tickets, backstage passes, and trips to see them play. A single multi-platinum, successful rock star could not have achieved that level of success without a backup band, studio personnel, record company support, radio airplay, and fans to buy the records.

No matter how hard you have worked for your success, you have to appreciate what you have and those that helped you achieve that success because, I promise you, you did not do it alone. Be grateful for everything that comes your way, appreciate all you have, and always realize that no one owes you a thing. From gifts and rewards to customers and vendors, to giving back to the community, to the always reliable thank you note, let others know that you appreciate their help along the way.

★ Light My Fire

Rock stars have to thank the record company and the radio personnel as well as remember to thank fans. Everybody in the food chain, above them and below them, is what makes for success. They award gold and platinum records to those employees in the company that they felt "worked" the record and made it a hit, and they award them to radio personnel as well. It's a nice perk to have on the wall. Rock stars also reward radio stations with free concerts and exclusive interviews. All of it says, "Thanks for making my record a hit. I couldn't have done it without you."

As a successful business owner, you should know that thanking customers is a given. But when is the last time you thanked your vendors? The Space Store not only sent gifts and notes to our best customers, but also to the vendors who supplied the items we sold. When we sent a chocolate tower to the shipping department of the astronaut patch company over the holidays, with a note to the staff, we knew our shipments would always get done right and sent out on time, if not early, all year long.

Billy Idol broke attendance records early one summer with a sold-out performance at the amphitheater in a local amusement park. Park management was so ecstatic at the bottom line that night that they rewarded Billy and his band by taking them to the water park next door after the show, opening the gift shop for bathing suits and towels and turning on some of the rides. It was a fun entourage to be included in, and I'll never forget the smell of wet hairspray from all the spiked hair and the running eye liner, a staple for rock bands in the '80s. It also made an impression in the back of my developing, entrepreneurial mind. Always thank the ones that make you the money.

And don't forget your employees. Whether it is with a bonus, a day off, or a gift certificate, you should reward a job well done. Yes, everyone should do their job correctly and do it to the best of their ability all the time. Yet, believe me, you can help that work ethic along with a little appreciation and make it consistent in your business. It's good for morale, and it's good for business.

★ Give a Little Bit

Look at the humanitarian work U2's Bono does around the world. This is not something he has to do. He was a rock star long before he started all this and could definitely sit back and rest on his laurels and large bank account. But do it he does, traveling the world, speaking to politicians on behalf of those less fortunate. And the side effects of such work aren't too shabby either. Bono has been nominated for the Nobel Peace Prize, was granted an honorary knighthood by the United Kingdom, and was named as a Person of the Year by Time.

Giving back to your community should be a given in your business, whether it is donating to a silent auction or volunteering your time. One of the best examples I've ever heard of was a company that gives their employees a set number of days off a year to volunteer for a charity. It's a paid day off that doesn't count against vacation or sick days, and it gives everyone in the company a sense of doing what is right. Karma may be a goofy word and still a little too metaphysical for some corporate executives, but whatever you want to call it, it pays off in morale for employees, reputation for the company, and a better life for others.

The KLOL Rock and Roll Auction comes up again and again in this book because it is an excellent example of marketing, networking, promotion, passion, and, most importantly, giving back to the community that put us on top. A lot of the celebrities that came through over the years and participated in the auction were smart enough to realize all of the above. It was not only a great opportunity for them to promote a new album or project, but it was also a great way to say thank you to the fans and to KLOL. A nice by product was all the press in the local papers and national trades.

I have been very fortunate in my various and assorted careers. When I first started in radio, I accepted every invitation to every charity event in Houston to emcee, appear, model, or whatever they needed me to do. The exposure was priceless and gained me more listeners each and every time. Over time, I was one of the highest-rated disc jockeys in Houston. Yet I continued to agree to every charity function request because it was the right thing to do. This community put me on top, I liked it there, and helping out was the least I could do.

★ We Will Rock You

After David Crosby served his time in the Texas prison system and was preparing to move into a Houston halfway house, I was contacted to see if I could help David with a dentist, local information, and more while he was in town. Although I did eventually get an amazing interview with David, there wasn't a guarantee or even an offer of an exclusive interview. There was nothing in it for me, but it was just the right thing to do, to help someone. David became a friend, introduced me to some friends he had made at NASA, who in turn introduced me to a NASA pilot by the name of Charlie Justiz. In real life, my legal name is Mrs. Charlie Justiz. It was an act of kindness that more than came back to me.

Doing something for no ulterior reason, other than to help another, is something else that should become a regular habit in your life. Introducing business associates without wanting in on the action, or passing on work you don't have time to do to a competitor, are the sorts of things that are remembered and come back to you tenfold later in business.

Kevin Hendon was a seventeen-year-old Van Halen fan in Houston as well as a cystic fibrosis patient. I had read about Kevin in the local paper and made arrangements for him to attend the upcoming Van Halen concert as a guest of the band. The band went so far as to make plans for a nurse and oxygen backstage for Kevin if it was needed. He was a very sick boy, but we were sure he would be out of the hospital in time for the show. Unfortunately, it did not work that way.

On the day of the show, Kevin was still very much in Texas Children's Hospital and was not going to be allowed to go to the show. He was just too sick. Van Halen cancelled everything they had planned that afternoon, jumped in their limos, and headed to the hospital to spend an hour with Kevin. No press and no ulterior motive. Just a visit with one thrilled teenage boy. We lost Kevin a couple of weeks after that. At his memorial, you could hear a recording of the Van Halen concert he had missed because the band had recorded the entire show for him. Van Halen stayed in heavy rotation on the radio station playlist and in my heart for a very long time after that generous act of kindness.

Never forget that you didn't do this alone. On your journey to the top, there are many people in all walks of life that help you reach the summit. Introducing these people to each other, passing on leads and work, and doing it all without wanting something in return will eventually deliver a return. You might not see the results immediately, but over time it starts to add up and you become known as a "go-to" person. Associates will not only remember you when they need something, but also when they have a lead or work for you.

★ The Letter

I was infamous, and sometimes laughed at, for the thank you notes I wrote in the rock and roll radio business. I would write a thank you note for concert tickets, backstage passes, trips, free records, mentions in the press, lunches, dinners. You name it, and I wrote a handwritten thank you note for it. Ronnie Raphael, one of the record reps at the time, once commented, "You would write a thank you note if someone held the door for you." Yep. Probably. Sure would.

Never underestimate the power of a handwritten thank you note. It is one of the most powerful tools in your business arsenal. It's simple, easy to do, inexpensive, one of the quickest things you'll do all day, and leaves a lasting impression with everyone. Yet hardly anyone does it anymore. Ever. Think about it. When was the last time you got a handwritten note thanking you for anything you have done?

> For the most part, I got along with everyone and enjoyed meeting everyone I had the opportunity to be around in the rock entertainment business. For some reason or another though, heartthrob Shaun Cassidy and I just did not hit it off the first time we met. I think we were both cocky and young, and I still wasn't sure he could cross out of his bubblegum image. A few days after our record company dinner, I received a handwritten note in the mail. I opened it and read, "Dear Dayna, Think of it this way. If you play the record, we won't have to see each other again. Things could be worse. Shaun Cassidy."
>
> I now use that note as an example of what not to write. I probably would have gone on to play the record if the note had been nicer. But hey, at least he took the time to write a handwritten note.

Each morning, one of the first things I do is think about the day before and the people I need to thank. Sometimes a follow-up call or e-mail is sent for an immediate communication, but I always follow that by something handwritten on my personal stationary and put in the mail. It has become somewhat of a signature piece for me, even though it is simply how I was raised. Make it a part of your routine and you'll make a lasting impression.

Appreciation

★ Reward a job well done

★ Give back to the community

★ Cultivate random acts of kindness

★ Write a thank you note

Encore

In Closing

★

"You ain't seen nothin' yet."

Bachman-Turner Overdrive

I ron Butterfly's "Inna Gadda da Vida" played as I
received my first kiss. I guess that should have been
a premonition that classic rock and roll would play a big
part in my life.

All of the stories in this book are true. At least it's the
way I experienced and perceived them. None of the names
have been changed to protect the innocent. None of us were
innocent. We were hip, we were cool, and we were having
the time of our lives. However, as I said before, I knew my
life as a female rock and roll disc jockey was short, and I had
better take full advantage of where I was, the opportunities I
was being given, and the people I was meeting.

For every story told in this book, there are dozens
more. It was an amazing time with incredible music that
still stands to this day as some of the greatest rock and

roll ever recorded. From WTAW and KAMU in Bryan/ College Station to KRBE and KLOL in Houston, I played music from the greatest rock bands to ever grace a stage or an album. And in every thing I have done since, I found I went back to things I learned during those great days in rock and roll radio.

I went on to thrive in television and talk radio. In 1998, I was named as one of *Talkers Magazine's 100 Most Important Talk Show Hosts*. I created and sold the Space Store, the largest online retailer, at the time, of NASA and other space related items. I also created, produced, and hosted *The Art of Doing Business* on the BizRadio Network in Houston and Dallas. Steele Media Services continues to operate as the umbrella company for my writing, speeches, and voiceover work. And my latest venture is Smart Girls Rock, an online community to encourage girls to pursue science, technology, engineering, math, medicine, and business.

Cristopher, my stepson, once asked me if there was anything in my life I regretted. "Yes," I said, without even having to think about it for a minute. "I regret not going to Berlin when I had a chance to dance on the Berlin Wall as it came down." Otherwise, every decision and action I stand by. Some good, some not so good, but I learned from all of it. And I really would have regretted not writing this book.

So, the time has come for you to create your own hit. You can start and grow a successful business. It's just a matter of taking all the elements and putting them together in the way that suits you. And best of all, your fate doesn't lie in the hands of a record company or band manager. It lies in your own, very capable hands.

I firmly believe that everyone has an idea for a successful business. Some have already taken action, some have expressed the idea, and others are not sure about letting the beast loose.

No matter where you are in the process, I hope you have learned some of the same lessons I learned while being entertained by some of the greatest rock stars, disc jockeys, and Steeleworkers in the world.

Rock on!

Equipment Manifest
Things I Can't Live Without

★

Treo Palm Mobile Phone

I can check and send e-mails, take calls, and keep up with the headlines. Then there are the pics of family, music, movies, and the occasional game my kids teach me how to play.

HP Pavilion Laptop

It's just an all-around good, sturdy, workhorse. Light-weight, I carry it everywhere, on planes, to meetings, cof-fee shops (where I wrote most of this book), and outside by the pool. Remember, on the Internet, no one knows you are a dog, *and* they don't know you are by the pool.

Small Blank Notebook and Pen

I almost always have these two items with me. I can jot fast notes, reminders, information, or give it to the kids for hangman in a restaurant. For such simple things, they sure are powerful.

iPod

I took my entire CD collection and downloaded every song into my iPod. There is stuff on there from Led Zeppelin, Aerosmith, ZZ Top, and others that I swear I never heard when the album actually came out. I try to walk every afternoon and look like an idiot playing air guitar. But it's great exercise.

Free Publicity by Jeff Crilley

I can't recommend this book enough to small businesses, non-profits, you name it. It is a small paperback written by a Dallas television reporter that solves the mystery of getting publicity. I even recommend it to my PR and marketing friends because sometimes going back and re-learning the basics will fuel even more creativity. www.jeffcrilley.com

Constant Contact

E-mail marketing software at an extremely reasonable price and easy to use. I first used this company with the Space Store and have used them for everything else since, including my current newsletter at www.daynasteele.com. It's a great way to keep in touch with customers and contacts. www.constantcontact.com

Café Press

This is another great service for small business. Café Press makes it so easy for a small business to offer branded products such as shirts, coffee mugs, mouse pads, and more. If this is your main business, then you obviously need to be using a wholesaler for better pricing. If you just want to be able to offer products with your brand or slogan but don't want the hassle of inventory and shipping, try www.cafepress.com. We host all Smart Girls Rock items on their site and it's a breeze.

The Emcee

Speaking Engagements

★

Dayna Steele is a popular speaker with groups of all sizes, ages, and backgrounds. Rock and roll is universal and enjoyed by all. Her speech topics range from these lessons learned from rock stars to starting a business, finding your passion, and more.

"Dayna was an inspiration to everyone who attended. Not only was she funny and inspiring, but she spoke about real life issues which we all deal with today, utilizing her great rock and roll background."

Kathy Snow, President
Professional and Support Staff Association

"Dayna Steele was the ideal speaker for our Meeting Planners International-Houston Area Chapter Women Leaders: Inside and Out Educational Series. Not only is she dynamic, charismatic, inspiring, and a truly admirable role model, she also knows exactly how to rock an audience. Our theme for the evening was "Smart Girls Rock," and no one represents that concept better than Dayna Steele."

Tracey Shappro, Senior Producer
VT2 Studios

"Yes! Yes! Yes! Dayna said exactly what we wanted the girls to hear, and tying attributes to rock bands and rock stars was brilliant."

Mary Ann Stanley, West Harris County Branch
American Association of University Women

"When we were searching for a keynote that could tap into the interests of young girls, we knew Dayna would be a perfect fit. Dayna had hundreds of sixth, seventh, and eighth grade girls on their feet! I continue to receive positive feedback about her motivational speech."

Elaina Polsen,
Community & Business Partnership Coordinator
Clear Creek Independent School District

"Dayna Steele is an entertaining and inspirational speaker. If you want your group to sit riveted in their chairs enjoying every minute and walking away with nuggets of good, useful information, then Dayna Steele is the lady to deliver your message. I would invite her back to speak in a heartbeat."

Kathryn Watson, Program Chair for CyFen
American Business Women Association

For booking information and availability:
Steele Media Services
info@daynasteele.com

About the Author
Dayna Steele

★

Dayna Steele, founder and creator of Smart Girls Rock, was one of the top female rock-and-roll air personalities in the country, was nominated as *1996 Local Radio Personality* by *Billboard Magazine,* and was also included in *Talkers Magazine's 100 Most Important Radio Talk Show Hosts, 1998.* Her radio broadcasts took her from the war zone in Bosnia to the opening of The Hard Rock Hotel in Las Vegas, to concerts and interviews with countless bands and rock stars around the world. On television, Steele anchored and reported for Houston Entertainment News, co-hosted a morning television show, and was the ring announcer for the Houston Boxing Association. In addition to her radio and television exploits, Steele also created the highly successful e-commerce venture, TheSpaceStore.com.

The T-Shirt Booth

Merchandising

★

ROCK TO THE TOP

If you would like to order additional copies of this book, they can be purchased online at

www.rocktothetopbook.com

Or you can send this form along with your payment to:

Steele Media Services

P.O. Box 72
Seabrook TX 77586

Number of books: _____ x $17.95　　　　= $ _____

Texas residents add 8.25% sales tax　　　　　　= $ _____
($1.48 per book)

S&H: _____ x $2.50 per book　　　　= $ _____

　　　　　　　　　　　　　　　TOTAL = $ _____

Shipping Address _____

City _____　　　State _____　　Zip _____

Billing Address _____

City _____　　　State _____　　Zip _____

Phone_____　　　　E-mail _____

Credit Card #_____　　Mastercard ☐　　Visa ☐　　Check ☐
　　　　　　　　　　　　　　　($25.00 returned check fee)

CVV# (3 digits on back)_____　　Expiration Date _____

Signature _____　　Date_____

Smart Girls Rock merchandise available at www.smartgirlsrock.com

Paparazzi

The Incriminating Photos

★

A rock and
roll diva in
the making.

In charge at WTAW-FM
in College Station.

At the controls at
Y94, my first taste
of rock and roll
radio. I was hooked.

My "attention getting" outfit for Disco 94, the dark ages of music.

My attempt at Texas Big Hair and the Zoolander look.

Shaun Cassidy   10/3/80

Dear Dayna —
think of it this way,
if you play the record
we won't have to see
each other again. things
could be worse...

The infamous "thank you" note from Shaun Cassidy

KISS's Peter Criss doing his stage makeup on my face for a Halloween promotion.

Eric Burdon of The Animals.
He used to call from the road
and I couldn't understand a
word he said with his accent.

Former police officer turned
rock star Eddie Money.

The famous KLOL Runaway Radio.

With Joan Jett at a KLOL
Rock and Roll Auction. We
were standing on the
counter at a record store.

That's me on the counter
behind Aerosmith's Steven
Tyler at the same KLOL
Rock and Roll Auction

Striking a pose with Stevie Ray Vaughan.

Trying to turn guitarist Jeff Beck into an honorary Texan.

Always suave and debonair, a young and handsome Rod Stewart.

This was the ad we did to welcome Bruce Springsteen to town, based on his Born To Run album cover.

Cheap Trick at my apartment after a show.

Legendary drummer Carmine Appice

A KLOL Rock and Roll Auction moment with
Richie Sambora and Jon Bon Jovi.

Guitarist Earl Slick, MTV's Martha Quinn and
David Letterman's Paul Shaffer helping with
an auction.

From The Police, hanging with Sting after a show.

Broadcasting live from Grammy Week Live in New York City with The Scorpions.

Jeff Watson and Brad Gillis of Nightranger at the KLOL Auction in the Houston Hard Rock Café's parking lot.

Hanging out on a piano with Bruce Hornsby.

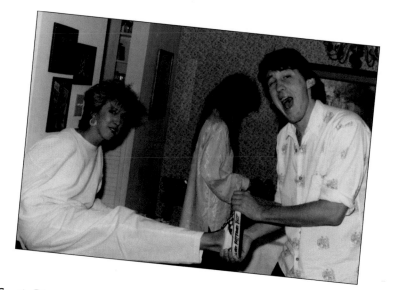

Fast Times at Ridgemont High creator Cameron Crowe. That's his wife Nancy Wilson of Heart in the background. I'm wearing the promo shoes from the movie.

Playing softball with Mötley Crüe.

The one and only Little Richard.

Making stage announcements at the Texxas Jam in front of 75,000 people.

John Kalodner: John Kalodner.

Van Halen visiting my friend Kevin
Hendon in the hospital.

DAYNA SIEGLE

VAN HALEN
ALIVE!
right here, right now.

NORTH
AMERICA
1993

VIP

WB

WORKING
PERSONNEL

DO NOT HUMP

NORTH
AMERICA
1993

AUG 3 1993

VAN HALEN LIVE:
right here, right now.

Radio

The late, great and always amazing
Ed Leffler, my mentor.

The billboard I hated.

One of the many gold and platinum albums
I received over the years. This one is for
Aerosmith's "Permanent Vacation."

My favorite Damn Yankees, Jack Blades and Tommy Shaw.

Crosby, Stills & Nash. They had just commandeered the radio station and taken over my show for an hour. Stephen Stills did the traffic reports!

Backstage with Charlie the Wonder
Husband and Billy Joel

My KLOL trading card.

A live broadcast with John Mellencamp who was always one of the best interviews.

NASA Space Shuttle Commander Tom Henricks listening to my show in space on STS-44.

David Crosby was a good friend for a long time. This has always been one of my favorite pictures.

Fleetwood Mac's Lindsey Buckingham helping me cut the ribbon at a KLOL Rock and Roll Auction in the building that is now home to Joel Osteen and Lakewood Church.

KISS's Gene Simmons helping me with an auction item.

Charlotte, the Parasailing Pig, makes daily appearances at the show. Clear Lake resident, boat enthusiast, and KLOL personality, Dayna Steele, broadcasts live from Watergate Yachting Center on October 1, from 10:00 a.m.-3:00 p.m.

An ad I keep handy to remind me that the pig got top billing.

The BBC's Mal Redding and Steve Howe of Yes and Asia fame relaxing at our house.

A bunch of sharply dressed men backstage, including ZZ Top's Frank Beard, Billy Gibbons, and Dusty Hill along with Charlie.

Backstage with The Rolling Stones. A typical
posed backstage shot!

The infamous Houston Health & Fitness take
on the Demi Moore and Vanity Fair pose.

Doing a live interview with Sammy Hagar
prior to a Van Halen show.

Leaving the stage at the KLOL Rock and Roll Auction. It was a great ride.